C000229158

Ciudad de México

EDSON DIAZ-FUENTES

Hardie Grant

BOOKS

Contents

Foreword

Growing up in rural France, in my small town of Tarbes, we ate the rustic dishes of Gascony. That was all we knew. So I can't claim a lifelong love of Mexican food. I was barely aware of the regional diversity of cooking even in France. It was only when I trained to be a chef, working in kitchens around the country, that I came fully to appreciate that the tastiest food often reflects the produce and traditions of a region.

A grandmother with no formal training can often produce dishes with more flavour than those of a classically trained chef, for all his or her finesse.

It was almost twenty years ago that I finally made it to Mexico, and it's fair to say my expectations were not high. I'd only tried Mexican food in London and it was not good. It feels like the English want chilli with everything. (It's the same with Indian food.)

I only spent a few days in Mexico City, but I'll never forget visiting a huge food market. I was surprised by the variety of vegetables and fruit. And there were sheets of crackling hanging from the ceiling. They would cut you a piece, weigh it, and you could walk along eating beautiful tasting food. Everything looked so good, and you could see that this was a country with a strong food culture, even if it wasn't quite so well-known overseas in those days.

We ate in *taquerias* and roadside stalls, and in more formal restaurants, too. It was then that I started to appreciate that Mexican cooking is more complex than people sometimes imagine. There's subtlety, and dishes are built with layers of flavour. Yes, some of those flavours are robust but, as with all good cooking, there is depth and there is balance. And there are colours, too. It's a cuisine where you can feast with your eyes.

My other fond memory is of my first visit to Santo Remedio. I love family-run restaurants, and the hospitality shown by Edson and his wife Natalie was second-to-none. There was warmth and there was joy so you felt happy even before the food arrived. When it did, it took me straight back to Mexico City.

I hope you enjoy this book as much as I do. For me, it brings back happy memories and also brings Mexico to life. While the focus is on Mexico City, it also points to the diversity of regional cuisines, so I guess I am going to have to return and do some exploring. For now, I find myself looking at recipes such as Smoky Cauliflower with *Pipián Blanco*; *Pibil*-style Pork Ribs; and Lamb Shanks, *Barbacoa*-style and I just want to get cooking. The recipes are accessible, even for a Frenchman.

Pierre Koffmann

Introduction

I have been a serious eater, or, as you would say in Mexico, a *tragón*, since the age of five. One of my earliest childhood memories was on holiday in Acapulco. The once-glamorous seaside spot was made famous in the 1950s when it was frequented by Hollywood film stars like Elizabeth Taylor and Ronald Reagan. It is where Mexico City's inhabitants would go at the weekends to escape the hustle and bustle of the city when I was a child in the early eighties.

I was at the *palapa* (stall) ready to enjoy breakfast, my favourite meal of the day. I was queueing where one of the cooks was preparing Mexican *antojitos* (corn-based snacks) on a comal (a Mexican flat-topped griddle). I stood there patiently, waiting my turn to order the black bean *sopes* I had decided on for breakfast. But adult after adult received their food while I was left waiting. What I hadn't realised what that the cook couldn't see me, as I was still so small. Though I didn't mind the being ignored. I was captivated.

I watched the cook roll round balls of *masa* (corn dough), placed them between two neatly cut plastic sheets and then press them in the tortilla press, forming perfectly round discs. She placed them carefully on the *comal* for just the right amount of time for them to cook, before pinching the edges to make them in to *sopes*. After which, they were smothered in black beans and topped with fresh cheese and cream.

Luckily, one of the other guests soon noticed me and ensured I received my *sopes*, and for the next few days the cook never failed to spot me again. I continued to enjoy the daily ritual, my perfect start to the day: the joy of watching and smelling fresh corn *masa* being cooked and popped on to my plate, and then the delight of devouring it at my table. You could say this marked the beginning of my culinary journey.

I was born and raised in Mexico City. It is chaotic, busy and always moving. It's a melting pot of flavours and food from across Mexico, one of the most biodiverse countries on this planet.

For me, as for all Mexicans, food is an integral part of life. There is no social gathering, festivity or event where food is not essential. Growing up in Mexico City, I was accustomed to regularly visiting its markets, street food stalls, *fondas*, cafes and, later, with my father José María, its *cantinas*.

What makes a cuisine so special and unique are not only the recipes, ingredients and

cooking techniques, but also the stories and traditions that surround the food. And, for me, so many of my memories are steeped in the food I grew up eating.

One of my favourite memories as a child was going shopping with my mother Lucero and sister Meri to Coyoacán Market. A task that was always rewarded by early morning quesadillas from a specific *puesto* (stand) that my mother used to like. Communal benches in the middle of the market were surrounded by *puestos*, offering a wide range of options, from tacos and *tostadas* to seafood and freshly squeezed juices. What we know today as artisanal food markets have been the norm in Mexico for centuries. That journey to Coyoacán to buy fresh produce for family meals was always accompanied by juices, freshly baked pastries and hot chocolate from different traders. It was a great way to start any morning and an impossible trip to resist.

Outings to Mexico's historic centre with my grandmother always included a visit to Churrería el Moro, which my mother and even my grandmother would visit as a child. Opened in 1935 by Spaniards fleeing the Civil War, it was a special treat for me to visit the famous *churrería*, watch the *churrero* pipe the dough into the boiling hot oil, and then emerge, crisp and light, moments later; to be dusted in sugar. Served piping hot on melamine plates and accompanied by a hot chocolate for dipping, they were the ultimate treat. Visits here were strewn with stories of my mother's childhood visiting her father's shops in the historic centre, which he had run for decades. Ultramarinos Canada was a shop which Abuelo Rafa ran for over thirty years. Probably it was one of the first shops in Mexico to sell the very best of Spanish produce, from olive oil to tinned sardines and *turrones*. After this, in 1968 he opened a sweet shop called *El Rey de las Cajetas*, selling hundreds of types of traditional Mexican sweets in De la Palma Street, Mexico's City Historic Centre.

Like this, there are an infinite number of culinary journeys that we had as a family, which I will never forget. Some kept evolving as we tried new and different foods, and some of them remained unchanged weekly rituals; we become loyal to those places, whether the local *taqueria*, torteria or traditional restaurants like El Arroyo on the outskirts of the city for a traditional *barbacoa*. It was here we would often go for impromptu celebrations with my family and my godparents Lili and Daniel, and their sons Daniel and Lalo, who were like brothers to me.

Even a simple roadside stand can evoke in me the most wonderful of memories. Like the *Milanesa torta* (a crispy schnitzel Mexican sandwich) stand outside high school in the south of Mexico City. They were delicious, filling and cheap, and you would eat them at the side of the stall for lunch. They were the ideal fuel for a student on a budget. I'm not sure if that stand exists anymore, but those wonderful *tortas* will forever punctuate those teenage years. Years spent rowing for the national rowing team, watching arthouse films at the Cineteca Nacional and eating my way around the city before leaving at the age of eighteen.

I was very lucky to grow up in a family and culture where good food was appreciated and available all year round. As I grew older, I learned to appreciate iconic restaurants in Mexico City – places like El Cardenal, Hacienda de Los Morales and El Bajio – which influenced my love and appreciation not only for great traditional food but also for impeccable hospitality.

I started cooking for groups of friends when my wife Natalie and I lived in a loft in Brooklyn, New York, back in 2010. I was inspired by the produce that was available in the *bodegas* in our neighbourhood, Bushwick, run by Mexican immigrants.

I began cooking at home, mixing flavours from my memories of family dishes and inspired by the regional street food of Mexico. I don't consider myself as someone who has a great visual memory, which is why I am always taking pictures of sights I want to remember. However, I do have a great taste memory. This has helped me a lot when recalling iconic dishes made by both my grandmothers, as well as the *puestos*, *fondas*, markets and, of course, restaurants of the fabulous and never-ending offering of Mexico City. These, combined with my travels, influence the food I create. From Baja California in the north of the country to the Yucatan in the south and my time spent doing a *stage* in the kitchen of one of Mexico's greatest chefs, Alejandro Ruiz of Casa Oaxaca in Oaxaca, which was immensely inspiring.

In 2014 Natalie and I moved to London, where we decided to set up Santo Remedio. Santo Remedio translates literally as 'holy remedy', an expression my mother often uses and which means a fortuitous or serendipitous solution to a problem. I wanted to share with Londoners the food I missed the most from markets, my home and family celebrations. We started off running pop-ups, supper clubs and market stalls before establishing our restaurant close to Tower Bridge. Carefully curated dishes, music, decor and service that can transport you to Mexico and make you feel happy is what we constantly strive to create. Whether it's the pork *carnitas* with salsa *verde* like those you can find in Mexico City, fish tacos inspired by Baja California or *huevos motuleños* from the Yucatan, all our dishes tell part of my story.

Many of the days writing this book were fuelled by foods delivered by local restaurants in Mexico City. As I write this, I am waiting for a delivery from La Barraca Valenciana, a Spanish *torteria* in Coyoacán in the south of Mexico City, famed for its market, picturesque square and La Casa Azul, home of Mexico's world-famous artists Frida Khalo and Diego Rivera.

It is December 2020 and, after almost twenty years living outside the city, vendors evoke once again the memories of my childhood. I had forgotten just how inextricably linked food and sound are in this city. Like an urban bird call, every vendor has their own unique siren.

The *camotes* vendor, who sells sweet potatoes roasted over charcoals and topped with condensed milk, and whose whistle is known to all; the person cycling from street to street shouting '*¡Tamales calientitos!*' (hot *tamales*), who I used to rush out to see as a child; there is the *esquites* cart, selling Mexico's most iconic ingredient, grilled or boiled corn kernels served with chilli powder, *queso fresco* or aged cheese, lime juice and mayonnaise, one of my favourite childhood snacks. Not forgetting the tacos *de canasta* sellers, whose unmistakeable bike horns can be heard around the streets at lunchtime.

Whether they be *tamaleros*, *camoteros*, *fruteros* or *chicharroneros*, all those who trade from the streets, visiting street by street, they would all bring a smile to my face as they came to my doorstep. Just as they still do – for the millions who live and worked in this sprawling city and for who the food is not only sustenance for the long hours worked, but also a moment of comfort and joy.

Santo Remedio ... COCINA MEXICANA
Santo Remedio
COCINA MEXICANA
¡Se habla español!
We also speak English

A Culinary Melting Pot

Mexico City is one of the world's biggest metropolises. There is a constant buzz and people are always on the move. The smell of street food being cooked up over charcoals, music blaring from buses and the notoriously bad traffic can all be an assault on the senses. But it is also beautiful, magical and surreal. With one of the biggest urban parks in the world, Chapultepec, and over 150 official museums, as well as beautiful architecture, murals, and colonial streets, it is a truly magnificent city – and that's before you even get to know its culinary wonders.

Known among Mexicans of my generation as DF – which stands for *Distrito Federal* – Mexico City is the capital of the country. It is a melting pot socially, economically, politically, and of the country's many culinary cultures.

People from the capital are known as *Chilangos*, and there is a magazine of the same name for locals. If you arrive by plane at night, the lights of the valley and surrounding mountains sprawling for miles below you are a truly magnificent sight. Like a gigantic golden jewel, a sea of gold, it goes on forever.

Mexico City's metropolitan area and surrounding states – Puebla, Estado de Mexico, Hidalgo, Tlaxcala and Morelos – create a gastronomic experience like no other, with an array of tastes and smells to delight the senses.

This metropolis of over 20 million hungry people is an unlimited maze of late night tacos stands, breakfast juice *puestos* and lunch *torta* stands. A monster that feeds hungry *Chilangos* three times a day, with something to eat on every corner and for every craving one might yearn for at any time of the day or night.

What you will find virtually everywhere you go are tacos. As I once said to someone who asked me when we eat tacos: tacos are a way of life. You simply can't separate a Mexican from a taco, as my dear friend Richard Ampudia says. And there is nowhere this is more true than in Mexico City, where you can enjoy a variety of tacos for breakfast, lunch or dinner – and at any time between. I enjoy trying all different kinds of tacos, from the traditional to the most inventive. Even though I believe there are no fixed rules for what you put in your tacos, I do think they have to work around three fundamental principles: tortillas, fillings and salsas.

According to Mexican chef and researcher Ricardo Munoz Zurita, the perfect taco can be eaten in three bites: just enough to satisfy your craving and leave you wanting more.

Nowhere is this better exemplified than In Mexico's historic centre at Los Cucuyos,

TAQUERIA
LOS COCUYOS
TACOS DE:

SURTIDA	$8.00
CAMPECHANO	$13.00
CABEZA	$13.00
MACIZA	$13.00
CACHETE	$13.00
OJO	$13.00
TRONCO DE OREJA	$13.00
MOLLEJA	$13.00
TROMPA	$13.00
TRIPA	$13.00
LONGANIZA	$13.00
SUADERO	$13.00
LENGUA	$15.00
SESOS	$15.00

which serves *tacos de cabeza* (beef head tacos.) It is a hole-in-the-wall that is open twenty-three hours a day, closing for just one hour in the middle of the night to clean and prep for the next day.

The tacos can be made with brains, ears, tongue, cheek or any other part of the head – not a single part is wasted. The bubbling pot of lard holds all the elements, which are chopped to order, served on two tortillas, as is customary in Mexico, and sprinkled with coriander, onion and salsa *verde*. They are incredibly tasty, with the mix of fat, spice and acidity creating a mind-blowing flavour with every bite.

But a tacos doesn't have to be simple, it can also be incredibly complex and refined. Pujol, which in 2019 made it to number twelve on The World's 50 Best Restaurants list has a tasting menu dedicated solely to tacos.

Before Pujol – and a few other contemporary restaurants – opened, many *Chilangos* regarded European cuisine, such as French or Italian food, as fine dining, with regional cuisine less highly regarded.

For many, this is the restaurant that put Mexico on the map as a culinary destination, and gave its cuisine the international recognition it deserved as one of the most complex, rich and fascinating in the world.

Just as it looks like the city is finally going to sleep, there is one place that starts coming to life. Trucks arrive from all over the country to fill almost thirty kilometres (eighteen miles) of aisles with fresh produce from all over Mexico. This is one of the biggest markets in the world, Mexico's Central de Abastos, which some would say is a city within a city.

It's an enormous market with its own banks, trading system, recreational areas, non-written rules and, of course, *taquerias* and food stands. It is a hub from which the entire city is fed. Everyone who runs a food business outlet, from fruit sellers to restaurateurs, and anyone whose business is selling or researching food, from photographers to anthropologists, will have visited the Central de Abastos.

Markets have always been central to our society. Our biodiversity and varied climate allows the *terroir* to produce a wide range of produce, from fruit and vegetables to coffee beans, cacao beans, vanilla beans – and more. In fact, Mexico introduced vanilla, cacao, avocados, tomatoes, corn and chillies to cuisines found around the world.

My recipes are a collection of the dishes I crave the most, made using the ingredients I treasure the most: cacao, corn, chillies and tomatoes, which I have combined with ingredients I have learned to love while living in the US and UK for the past fifteen years. Many of my recipes, like the *Padrón Rajas con Crema* (page 182) or my Spicy Chocolate *de Agua* (page 108) are a product of this integration of ingredients. I don't like to feel too restricted, and really enjoy adapting recipes to suit the local fresh produce.

Starting the day with *Atole de Fresas* (page 122), and French Toast with Agave, Cacao Nibs and Bacon (page 120) might not sound very traditional, but for me it has elements of Mexican dishes, combined with the best of English ingredients like its unrivalled sweet strawberries. It's my version of the *atole* drink enjoyed for centuries by Mexicans. French toast with bacon and agave used to be my father's treat for a Saturday morning – so it simply had to be included it in this cookbook.

This book has been inspired by a leisurely weekend in Mexico City, with the types of dishes you would eat at different times of day and which evoke a sense of the city at that time of day – whether enjoying a good book on an early morning while sipping coffee and eating a pastry in La Roma; enjoying early evening drinks in the picturesque historic neighbourhood of La Condesa; or a late night in one of the iconic *cantinas* of the historic centre listening to *mariachis* after visiting the impressive Art Deco concert hall at Palacio de Bellas Artes. As the stories in the subsequent chapters show, there is always a time of day or night when the food and drinks of Mexico City have something to offer.

The Pillars of Mexican Cooking

Before it was known as Mexico City, Tenochtitlan was the ancient capital of the Aztec empire founded in around 1325 on Lake Texcoco. It is believed that the city was founded by a group of Nahua tribes who, according to legend, decided to settle where they saw an eagle perched on a cactus on a lake. As the legend goes, this was the lake on which Mexico City is now built.

Mexico City is located in a valley surrounded by mountains and volcanoes – the most iconic ones are Popocatépetl and Iztaccihuatl. Centuries ago, it was made up of many adjoining canals that connected the markets and different areas of this bustling city, with boats transporting both people and goods from across the territory. At the time of the Spanish invasion it was bigger and cleaner than any city in Europe. These markets, known as *tianguis*, were the centres of both society and commerce. To this day, the city's markets are an integral part of its social and economic fabric.

One of the most important areas of the city for me is Xochimilco, which pre-dates the Spanish conquest and has, remarkably, survived to this day. It has an elaborate system of *chinampas*, linked by waterways.

The word *chinampa* comes from the Náhuatl word *chinámitl*. *Chinampas* were built in prehispanic times to grow crops by piling up mud from the bottom of the lakes in the Valley of Mexico to create small rectangular areas of fertile land divided by canals. The mud is extremely rich in organic matter and is kept in place by creating a fence with pieces of wood. The soil absorbs water and nutrients by filtration so is not dependent on rain or the seasons. This technique converts land some would consider unusable into an extremely productive food system.

Between 1400 and 1600 CE, the *chinampas* were at their peak in Tenochtitlan, and over eighty different types of plants were grown. However, some researchers say that this 'technology' has been use for centuries – if not millennia.

These incredibly fertile plots of land are used to this day to grow corn, tomatoes, beans, chillies and other products that are then sold in the city's markets. What makes these man-made areas of land so extraordinary is that they are so rich in nutrients that they can be harvested three times a year. The traditional method of crop rotation for the *chinampas* is still used to this day. Sadly, the expansion of the city and a lack of appreciation for this traditional method of growing means Xochimilco is in danger of dying out. Considering the *chinampas* survived an invasion and subsequent conquest, this would, represent an immensely tragic end to the type of technology this planet needs now, more than ever.

The cuisine of Mexico City is made up of a mixture of indigenous ingredients and dishes and produce bought to Mexico by the Spanish conquest in 1521. This is when pork, chicken, beef and lamb, as well as dairy products, were introduced to Mexico, then known as the New Spain. Many ingredients also came from Asia via the Phillipines and from Africa and the Middle East because of the Moorish conquest of Spain. Mexico, in turn, exported chillies, chocolate, vanilla, corn, tomatoes and avocados, among other ingredients.

In the late 1930s, because of the Spanish Civil War, many Spanish artists, professionals and others looking to flee, found in Mexico a welcoming new home. In turn they brought with them their culture, vitality and culinary traditions, introducing them to Mexican society through restaurants and grocery shops. This included restaurants, grocery shops and traditional dishes. There are still many Spanish-style *cantinas*, like Covadonga and El Sella, whose menus offer classic Spanish dishes including *chamorros*, *morcilla* or *pescado a la sal*. They have been served in the city for so long, they are an integral part of Mexico's cuisine.

Bacalao a la vizcaina is one such dish. It represents the fusion of Spanish heritage and Mexican cooking, adapted and adopted by Mexico City's inhabitants in around the 1950s. This dry and salted fish, cooked with tomatoes, onions, parsley and chillies, is now the classic Christmas dish enjoyed by virtually every family in Mexico City at Christmas.

Lebanese immigrants, who arrived in the 1920s and 1930s, bought their shawarma-style kebabs, which were again adapted using Mexican chillies, pork instead of lamb, and tortillas instead of pitta bread – and so tacos al pastor were born. They are now served in the hundreds of *taquerias* that are dedicated to this one dish.

Traditional Mexican food was declared an Intangible Cultural Heritage of Humanity by UNESCO in 2010 due to the diversity and complexity of the cuisine, as well as the history of many of the dishes. For those of us who have dedicated our lives to sharing these dishes, the ten-year anniversary of this declaration marked a growing worldwide appreciation of what the late Anthony Bourdain once described as "one of the most underrated, misunderstood and under-represented of all cuisines." But thanks to the work of researchers like Diana Kennedy, who has dedicated decades researching Mexican ingredients, recipes and cooking techniques well in to her 90s, more people are understanding the complexities of this cuisine outside of Mexico.

The pillars or roots of Mexican cooking are traditionally based on corn or maize, beans and, of course chillies, including all their possible variations. There are over one hundred varieties of corn – heirloom corn – that varies in form, colour and flavour. Blue corn, for example, is often used while preparing *antojitos* Mexicanos (corn snacks) and, when available, I would choose it over the traditional yellow corn for a more earthy flavour. There is also red, purple and even black corn, all with different flavour profiles and textures. Popping corn is native to Mexico, too, so every time you have popcorn, you are basically enjoying Mexican food. As is the case with amaranth and chia: these so-called 'superfoods' are ancient grains consumed for centuries by Mexican families.

For me, cooking is not only a survival activity of transforming food like our ancestors, it's a pleasure, turned into a passion, turned into a profession.

When we cook, we build flavour profiles as we incorporate ingredients. I would probably say that one misconception many have about Mexican food is that the savoury dishes have to be spicy. We certainly use chillies in the majority of our dishes, most importantly *adobos*, *moles*, *recaudos* or marinades. However, in cooking, as in life, balance is key. When mixing different flavours, including chillies, we consider and balance tastes like saltiness, sweetness, sourness, bitterness and umami – the mission of chillies is to enhance flavour. They are also good for our immune system.

Aztecs and Mayans used to combine cacao and chilli with water to make a delicious ceremonial drink that provided nutrients but also kicked endorphins into the body. Ultimately, chillies were considered to have medicinal purposes, being good for the metabolism and general health.

When cooking at home, I really hope you can incorporate some personal touches into the majority of the basic recipes in this cookbook, especially those from the Basics chapter (pages 40–73) and the Marinades, Rubs & Salsas chapter (pages 74–99). As you get used to the recipes, you can tweak according to your family's preferences.

Key for the success of any recipe are good-quality, in-season ingredients, as well as love when preparing the food. The majority of the dishes in this cookbook are broken down into sub-recipes, meaning some components can be prepped in advance to save time, and adapted as needed. They are structured just like at our restaurant, Santo Remedio, making it easier for you to prep in advance for yourself, family or friends. For example, *Caldillo de Jitomate* (page 51) is so versatile,

it can be used as a base for *Sopa de* Tortilla (page 144), *Huevos Motuleños* (page 136) or Hibiscus Flower Enchiladas (page 153), and can be prepped in advance. It can also build something more complex if combined with other components like Chipotles *en Adobo* (page 82), Salsa *de* Árbol (page 92) and Guajillo *Adobo* (page 89). These, in addition to pickles, salsas, marinades, ketchup and *chamoy* can become part of your new seasonal family cooking essentials.

The aim of this cookbook is to inspire you rather than to impose on you the tyranny of following recipes to the letter. Ultimately, it is the pleasure of cooking and feeding others that inspires us to cook for our family and friends. So I encourage you to be creative. There is no need to feel limited if you cannot find a particular ingredient: you can use the fish of your preference; opt for meco chipotle chillies instead of morita; or use Thai green chillies if it's not possible to source green jalapeños. It is just a question of keeping the balance by understanding each ingredient – and that is only achieved by cooking and tasting, more cooking and more tasting.

Let me warn you that preparing good *masa* dough requires time and patience. I hope you will enjoy making *tamales* like we do at home, and that you can have fun making the ones from my recipes. You can also create new variations of *tamales* by incorporating leftover Sunday roast meats or stews, which can easily be wrapped in corn *masa* dough and steamed. This cookbook is not focused on traditional recipes. Instead, the purpose of it is to encourage you to discover new flavours at home while learning about new ingredients and techniques from Mexican cuisine.

BASICS

Bases

Chiles en Escabeche

You will see big jars of these pickles in *torterias* and *fondas*. You can really taste all the flavours from the spices, but they are not too spicy. When preparing my pickles, I like combining layers of flavours by using aromatics like coriander seeds, honey and smoky dried chillies. Enjoy them in your favourite *torta* or sandwich, or enjoy them with Tacos *de Canasta* (page 165) and a beer.

MAKES 2 X 1-LITRE (34-FL OZ) JARS

180 g (6½ oz) baby potatoes, halved
1 litre (34 fl oz/4 cups) water
250 ml (8½ fl oz/1 cup) cider vinegar
3 tablespoons honey
1 tablespoon coriander seeds
1½ teaspoons salt
2 pasilla mixe chillies (dried morita or meco chipotle chillies can also work)
4 bay leaves
90 g (3¼ oz) baby carrots, halved
100 g (3½ oz) baby corn, halved
250 g (9 oz) green or red jalapeño chillies

1. Place the potatoes in a large saucepan of boiling salted water. Place over a high heat and boil for 10 minutes or until tender, then drain.

2. Place the water, vinegar, honey, coriander seeds, salt, pasilla mixe chillies and bay leaves in a large non-reactive saucepan over a medium heat. Bring the mixture to a simmer and cook for 10 minutes. Add the potatoes to the pan along with the carrots, corn and jalapeños and remove from the heat. Let it cool down for 10 minutes.

3. Divide the vegetables between the two jars, then top up with pickling liquid. The pickles will be ready to eat the next day and will keep in the refrigerator for up to 1 month.

TIP: An easy way to sterilise the jars is to put them in a preheated oven at 170°C/150°C fan/340°F/gas mark 3½ for 20 minutes. Remove from the oven and leave to cool.

Mojo de Ajo

Mojo de ajo is the secret to easy Mexican cooking. Once cooked and stored in the refrigerator, it becomes the ready-made base ingredient for *guisados* and *adobos*, and perfect for vegetarian *refritos* like the Avocado Black Bean *Refritos* (page 71). The garlic cloves are slowly confited in oil, acquiring a unique caramelised flavour which is a seasoning in itself.

MAKES 300 G (10½ OZ)

300 g (10½ oz) garlic cloves, peeled (see Tip)
about 200 ml (7 fl oz/scant 1 cup) grapeseed oil
¼ teaspoon fine sea salt

1. Place the garlic cloves and oil in a small saucepan, making sure the garlic are completely covered, almost submerged. Add a bit more oil if needed. Place the saucepan over a medium heat and bring to a simmer, then reduce the heat to low and cook slowly for 30 minutes until the garlic cloves turn golden-brown. They should be soft and break easily.

2. Remove from the heat and allow to cool. Add the salt and check the seasoning.

3. Once cool, use a hand-held blender to blend the garlic to a smooth paste, making sure any excess oil is properly emulsified into the mixture. You will find that smaller batches tend to separate slightly, which is absolutely fine.

4. The *mojo de ajo* will keep in a glass container in the refrigerator for a couple of weeks.

NOTE: For a bigger batch of *mojo de ajo*, place the garlic and oil in an ovenproof container and roast at 160°C/140°C fan/325°F/gas mark 3 for 45 minutes–1 hour, until the garlic cloves are soft and golden-brown. Remove from oven, season with salt and allow to cool before blending.

TIP: To peel the garlic cloves, halve them first. The peel will then detach easily. Using the tip of the knife, remove the bitter germ from the centre.

Onion Sofrito

As with the *Mojo de Ajo*, I like to make a large batch of this and keep it in the refrigerator. Once you have it, making other recipes becomes a lot quicker and easier. Adding the garlic paste intensifies the flavour of the onion and the emulsion of onion, garlic and oil acts as a natural thickener.

MAKES 350 G (12 OZ)

150 g (5 oz) *Mojo de Ajo* (page 49)
500 g (1 lb 2 oz) onions, finely sliced
½ teaspoon fine sea salt

1. Heat the *Mojo de Ajo* in a medium-sized sauté pan over a low heat. When it's hot and sizzling, add the onions. Stir for a few minutes making sure all the onion slices are well coated with *Mojo de Ajo*, then reduce the heat to low and simmer gently for 20 minutes. Keep an eye on the onions, stirring and scraping the bottom of the pan regularly, and checking to make sure they cook evenly and nothing catches or burns.

2. When the onions are soft and slightly golden, add the salt and stir well, then take off the heat and leave to cool.

3. It will keep in a glass container in the refrigerator for 4–5 days.

Caldillo de Jitomate

One of the first memories I have of my *Abuela* Carmela is her cooking this. It is the base for so many *guisados*, like *Chiles Rellenos* (page 220). I believe each family has its own recipe, with plenty of variations. You can use this *caldillo de jitomate* for *motuleños* and *enchiladas*. It is ideal for introducing Mexican cooking to your kids: I make it this way at home because my kids can't handle spice yet, and it's the perfect base for a non-spicy *Sopa de* Tortilla (page 144).

I do, however, like to add chillies for a deeper flavour. Dried or smoked chillies – ancho, mulato, chipotle, meco – will add some richness. Toast them in a *comal* or heavy, non-stick frying pan, pressing them down with a spatula, until they are soft and pliable. Be careful not to burn them. Simply add these to the *caldillo* when reducing.

**MAKES 1.3 LITRES
(44 FL OZ/5¼ CUPS)**

1.5 kg (3 lb 5 oz) ripe plum
    tomatoes, quartered
2 red onions, quartered
60 g (2 oz) garlic cloves, peeled
200 ml (7 fl oz/scant 1 cup) water
50 g (2 oz) *Mojo de Ajo* (page 49)
4 bay leaves
6 dried avocado leaves
1½ teaspoons salt
½ teaspoon freshly ground black
    pepper
brown sugar or agave syrup, to
    taste (optional)

1. Place the tomatoes and onions in a blender or food processor. Add the garlic cloves and about 50 ml (1¾ fl oz/3 tablespoons) of the water. Blend well in order to obtain a smooth purée.

2. Place a large, heavy-based saucepan or pot over a medium heat. Add the *Mojo de Ajo*, bay leaves and avocado leaves, and fry for a few minutes to release some flavour. Pour in the blended tomato mixture and stir until mixed properly. Add the rest of the water and mix well again. Bring to a simmer, then cook over a low heat for 20–25 minutes, until its colour changes to a deep red. Stir occasionally during this time, making sure nothing catches on the bottom of the pan.

3. Season with salt and pepper, and a bit of brown sugar or agave syrup if you need to balance the acidity. Use the sauce straight away, or leave to cool. It will keep in an airtight container in the refrigerator for up to 4 days.

Cebolla Morada

These sharp, citrusy pickled onions carry a hint of sweetness that cuts well through rich, fatty meats. They are ideal for *cochinita pibil*, one of my favourite Yucatecan dishes, but also work well in salads, as garnishes and more.

MAKES A 1-LITRE (34-FL OZ/1 CUP) JAR

200 ml (7 fl oz/scant 1 cup) lime juice
100 ml (3½ fl oz/scant ½ cup) orange juice
150 ml (5 fl oz/scant ⅔ cup) cider vinegar
20 g (¾ oz/5 teaspoons) caster (superfine) sugar
2 teaspoons salt
½ teaspoon Mexican oregano
500 g (1 lb 2 oz) red onions, halved and finely sliced

You will need a 1-litre (34-fl oz) glass jar

1. In a jug (pitcher), combine the lime juice, orange juice, cider vinegar, sugar and salt. Stir well until the sugar and salt are dissolved. Add the oregano and stir once again.

2. Place some of the onion slices into the jar and pour over some of the citrus brine. Press down on the onions with a wooden spoon to compress them. Add more onion slices and citrus brine, and press down again. Continue in this way until the onions are well compacted and the jar is full.

3. Make sure the onions remain submerged and leave to pickle for 48 hours in the refrigerator, shaking the jar every so often. After this time, they'll be ready to use, but they will keep in the refrigerator for up to a month.

Hibiscus Cordial

Hibiscus flowers are high in antioxidants and vitamin C. I use the reserved cooked flowers left in this recipe to make a plant-based filling for quesadillas, enchiladas or empanadas, pan-frying them with *Mojo de Ajo* (page 49), *Caldillo de Jitomate* (page 51) and a touch of *Chipotles en Adobo* (page 82). Not all hibiscus flowers are edible, though, so see page 176 for more details.

MAKES 1.5 LITRES (53 FL OZ/6 CUPS) CORDIAL AND 250 G (9 OZ) COOKED FLOWERS FOR USE IN OTHER RECIPES

100 g (3½ oz) hibiscus flowers
1.5 litres (53 fl oz/6 cups) water
350 g (12 oz/1¾ cups) caster (superfine) sugar

1. Carefully wash the flowers under running water to remove any sand, stones or dirt stuck between the petals.

2. Place the water in a large saucepan over a medium heat and bring to the boil. Add the flowers and cook for 10–15 minutes, stirring constantly, until the flowers are soft but still firm and have released all of their flavour and colour into the water.

3. Remove the flowers with a skimmer or slotted spoon and set aside for use in another recipe. When all the flowers have been removed, add the sugar to the saucepan and stir until dissolved. Leave to simmer for 10–15 minutes, until slightly syrupy.

4. Leave to cool, then bottle up and keep in the refrigerator for up to 2 weeks.

Hibiscus Compote

This compote retains all the antioxidants and vitamin C of the hibiscus, and is delicious spooned over pancakes or Amaranth and Coconut Porridge (page 139).

MAKES 400 G (14 OZ)/SERVES 6

50 g (2 oz) dried hibiscus flowers
500 ml (17 fl oz/2 cups) water
1 cinnamon stick
5 g (⅛ oz) fresh ginger root, peeled and thinly sliced
200 g (7 oz/1 cup) jam sugar
50 ml (1¾ fl oz/3 tablespoons) orange juice

1. Place the water, cinnamon and ginger in a medium-sized saucepan over a high heat and bring to the boil.

2. Meanwhile, carefully wash the hibiscus flowers under running water to remove any sand, stones or dirt stuck between the petals. Drain well.

3. Add the washed dried flowers to the pan, along with the sugar. Stir well for 5 minutes to help dissolve the sugar and release maximum flavour and colour into the water.

4. Reduce the heat to medium and simmer for about 30 minutes, until the flowers become glassy and the sauce is syrupy. Add the orange juice at the end.

5. Transfer to a bowl and serve warm or at room temperature. This compote will keep in the refrigerator for a few weeks.

Corn *Masa* for Tortillas

Nixtamalisation is an ancient cooking technique developed by Mesoamerican cultures over 3,000 years ago. This process involves the dry corn being soaked and cooked in an alkaline solution, making it more digestible and nutritious while removing impurities. It is then ground, traditionally in *molinos* (mills) all over Mexico. This technique produces the perfect dough consistency, malleable enough to be pressed and turned into a tortilla, one of the most common uses of this dough (although it is also the base for all *antojitos Mexicanos*, including *sopes, huaraches, gorditas*, etc.). This fresh dough is what you will see in Mexican markets next to the tortilla presses or traditional *tortillerias*.

Corn *masa harina* is made from dried corn that has been nixtamalised and then dehydrated. By simply adding water, we can make the *masa* dough and turn it into tortillas.

Mexico's diversity has been key in developing over 100 varieties of heirloom and indigenous corn that are delicious, nutritious and endemic to specific regions. White and yellow corn are the most commonly found across the country, but my favourite is blue corn. I remember having the option to choose between yellow and blue corn when I was a child in Mexico City while ordering *antojitos* from my local street stand: I always chose blue corn quesadilla, fresh from the *comal*.

To make tortillas, you need a tortilla press, a tool that is easily available online. Making and cooking tortillas requires practice. You need to understand the consistency of the dough. If it's too dry, it will produce a dry tortilla; if it's too wet, it will fall apart. Smaller tortillas are used for tacos, large ones for enchiladas and quesadillas. Extra-large ones, measuring 60 cm (24 in) are used for a relatively new *antojito* made in Mexico City called *machetes*, which are essentially very long quesadillas filled with the stew – *guisado* – of your choice.

The second important tool you will need is what we call the *comal*. The best ones are made of clay, but a cast-iron pan or a heavy non-stick frying pan (skillet) will do the trick. The perfect tortilla is cooked on a high enough heat to allow it to puff up slightly with just a few little brown spots.

250 g (9 oz/2¼ cups) corn *masa harina* (white or blue)
about 300 ml (10 fl oz/1¼ cups) lukewarm water
½ teaspoon salt
1 tablespoon vegetable oil

1. Place the *masa harina* in a large bowl.

2. In a jug (pitcher), combine the lukewarm water and salt and stir until the salt is completely dissolved. Add the vegetable oil and mix.

3. Make a well in the centre of the *harina* and start adding the water in stages. Add some of the water, then start mixing with your hand. Continue mixing as you add more water, until all the *harina* has been incorporated and a dough forms. Take your time to mix, slowly adding the water and familiarising yourself with the dough's consistency. It should have a smooth consistency with no lumps, and it should not stick to your hand. It should feel like playdough. If the dough becomes too wet, add more dry *masa harina*. If the dough is too dry and crumbly, add a little more water. Taste to check the seasoning and adjust accordingly if a bit more salt is needed.

4. Wrap the dough in cling film (plastic wrap) or a damp tea towel and allow to rest for 10 minutes before using.

MAKES ABOUT 15 TORTILLAS FOR TACOS

1 quantity of *masa* for tortillas (see above)

To make tortillas

1. Heat a *comal* or non-stick frying pan (skillet) over a medium heat.

2. Take 30 g (1 oz) dough from the *masa*. Roll it into a ball in your hand until smooth, then place inside the tortilla press between the two sheets of plastic. Close the press and apply pressure. You should get a 10-cm (4-in) disc. We call that a *tortilla taquera*, which is the norm for Mexico City street food.

3. Place the disc of dough on the *comal* or frying pan and cook for about 1 minute or until the edges start to dry. Flip it and leave for a couple of minutes, until tiny specks appear on the surface and puff up slightly. The first tortilla will help you test the heat of your pan. Adjust accordingly. Once cooked, place your tortillas inside a folded tea towel to keep warm and continue with the remaining dough.

4. You can make bigger tortillas, of course, by using more dough, with 15-cm (6-in) corn tortillas being what we normally find sold by the kilo in *tortillerias*. This is the most traditional tortilla size, and they are served for lunch or dinner with our traditional *guisados*.

MAKES ABOUT 30 *SOPES*

1 quantity of *masa* for tortillas (see above)

To make *sopes*

Use 20 g (¾ oz) balls of *masa* and roll them in your hand until smooth. Using a tortilla press, flatten each one into an 8 cm (3¼ in) disc about 0.5 cm (¼ in) thick. Cook on the heated *comal* or frying pan (skillet) for about a minute on each side. They should be slightly undercooked. Remove from the pan and, while they are still warm, pinch the sides between your thumb and index finger to form little pies with raised edges.

TIP: To reheat shop-bought tortillas, apply a light coating of oil onto each side of a tortilla and pan-fry 30 seconds on each side. Fat always helps and improves everything, and tortillas are no exception. It also enhances the corn flavour by caramelising the surface. *Taqueros* dip their tortillas in oil, melted fat or chorizo oil from the *plancha* before reheating. Wrap in a folded kitchen towel and serve straight away.

Corn *Masa* for Savoury *Tamales*

My earliest memory of *tamales* is when I was in kindergarten and my mum would get *tamales* for lunch from the lady around the corner on the way to school. I used to get really disappointed when the lady wasn't there as that meant my school lunch would be incomplete. For us Mexicans, *tamales* are not just street food: they are part of our heritage and strongly connected to family celebrations like birthdays, in addition to national celebrations like *Día de la Candelaria*.

I remember the preparations for these celebrations: my grandmother, *abuela* Carmela, standing next to the table in the kitchen all day long, filling and folding *tamales* traditionally in corn husks, with the irresistible smells of corn *masa* and *mole* in the air. My grandma's best *tamales* were filled with chicken and *mole*, but wrapped in chard leaves instead of corn husks. The chard leaves and the filling cooked at the same time, so the *tamales* was ready to eat as soon as it comes out of the steamer, and you didn't need to let it sit as you would for a corn husk *tamales*.

Tamales are usually filled with pork and chicken, but vegetable fillings like *poblano rajas*, squash or black beans are also used. A special mention must go to the sweet *tamales* found in Mexico City, with the strawberry and pineapple ones being the most popular. I hope you enjoy my recipe for Hibiscus *Tamales* (page 124) and perfect the technique as you enjoy sweet and savoury fillings.

As with tacos, an essential part of savoury *tamales* is the salsa or *adobo*: traditionally, salsa *verde* for pork, and *mole* for chicken. I believe these are *Chilangos'* favourite *tamales*.

MAKES 12

325 g (11½ oz/3 cups) corn
  masa harina
1 teaspoon baking powder
about 450 ml (15 fl oz/1¾ cups)
  lukewarm water
8 g (⅓ oz) salt
190 g (6¾ oz) goose fat or lard,
  melted and lukewarm

1. Place the *masa harina* in a large bowl. Add the baking powder and whisk until well blended.

2. Combine the lukewarm water and salt in a jug (pitcher) and stir until the salt is completely dissolved.

3. Make a well in the centre of the *harina*. Start by adding the fat, then begin mixing with your hand, slowly adding the water as you do so. Continue to mix until a dough forms with a smooth consistency and no lumps. It should be soft and slightly sticky. Work this dough well, for at least 7 minutes, until it becomes light and very malleable. You can use a stand mixer for this or ideally a thermal mixer. Taste to check seasoning and adjust accordingly.

4. Wrap in cling film (plastic wrap) or a damp kitchen towel and allow to rest for 10 minutes before using.

MAKES 12

12 large dried corn husks (see Tip)
820 g (1 lb 12 oz) *masa* for *tamales*
(see left)
360 g (12¾ oz) cooked chicken,
pork or stewed meat
360 ml (12 fl oz/scant 1½ cups)
Salsa *Verde* (page 88), Salsa *Roja*
(page 78) or *mole* of your choice

To make *tamales*

1. Place the corn husks in a large saucepan of simmering water and leave to soften for 30 minutes.

2. Fill the bottom of a steamer with water to a depth of 5 cm (2 in) and bring to the boil.

3. To make a *tamale*, place 65 g (2¼ oz) *masa* in the centre of one of the softened corn husks. Spread out the *masa* and place 30 g (1 oz) meat in the centre, then spoon 2 tablespoons of your chosen sauce over the meat. Fold the edges of the *masa* over the filling to form a tube. Tuck both ends of the tube in towards the centre and secure with a strand of husk or a piece of string. If the corn husk is not long enough for this, tie each end like a Christmas cracker. Repeat with the remaining ingredients to make 12 *tamales*.

4. Cook the *tamales* in the steamer for 25 minutes, then turn off the heat and leave in the steamer for another 25 minutes. Unfold and serve the *tamales* in their husks, but do not eat the husks – just use them as plates, then discard.

TIP: If your corn husks aren't big enough, you can use two overlapping husks for each *tamale*.

Wheat Tortillas

Wheat is not indigenous to Mexico. It was introduced through colonisation, but is now widely grown and used for tortillas, empanadas, *teleras*, *bolillos*, *buñuelos* and pastries. Corn tortillas need to be pressed, because of their lack of gluten, but wheat tortillas are rolled. They are usually made with lard, but I find that goose fat, which melts at a higher temperature than lard, gives the tortillas a smoother texture and a better flavour. There is a knack to rolling a tortilla. It is important to flip it over after each roll so that it is stretched on both sides. Cook them as soon as they are rolled, as they will dry out quickly and start to crack.

I have fond memories of visiting my *Abuela* Josefina when I was a child in Mexico City. She would cook freshly made wholewheat tortillas for breakfast with *huevos a la Mexicana* early on Saturday mornings for my father, my cousin Armando and me. Exciting for a *tragón* (eater).

MAKES 6 TORTILLAS

420 g (14¾ oz/scant 3¾ cups) plain
   (all purpose) flour,
   plus extra for rolling
⅛ teaspoon baking powder
1 teaspoon salt
70 g (2½ oz) goose fat, melted
about 200 ml (7 fl oz/scant 1 cup)
   warm water

1. Place the flour, baking powder and salt in a bowl. Whisk until well blended.

2. Make a well in the centre of the flour. Add the fat and begin mixing with your hand, slowly adding the water a little at a time. Continue to mix until a soft dough forms. Set aside for 5 minutes to allow the flour to absorb the liquids.

3. After resting the dough, knead it for 10 minutes until stretchy and smooth. This step is important as it will enable you to roll the dough thinly. Wrap in cling film (plastic wrap) and set aside for 1 hour.

4. Separate the dough into 6 pieces. Roll each one into a ball and set aside, covered. Lightly dust the kitchen counter with flour. Flatten each ball into a disc, then roll it out until very thin. Start rolling from the centre, away from you first, then towards you. Lift and flip over, giving the dough a quarter turn, then roll again. Dust with more flour if needed. Continue rolling and flipping until you have a thin disc about 30 cm (12 in) in diameter.

5. Heat a large frying pan (skillet) over a medium–high heat. Add the first tortilla to the pan and cook for about 1½ minutes. You will see little bubbles appear around the edges, then in the centre. Turn and cook on the other side for about another minute. The tortilla should be pliable and soft. If it feels stiff, it is overcooked. Wrap in a kitchen towel to keep warm, and repeat with the remaining tortillas.

Telera Bread

These are the traditional buns for *tortas*, the famous Mexican hot or cold sandwiches. Often baked in *panaderías* early in the morning, their soft texture makes it easy to bite through the generous filling of a *torta* or a *pambazo*. When rolling the *telera*, make sure you are stretching the dough well. The stretch and the grooves of the parallel lines will ensure a flat bun rather than a puffed-up roll.

There is one *torteria* in Mexico City that has been my family's favourite for years: El Rey del Pavo in the historic centre of the city. These guys have been selling *tortas* for over 110 years, so they must know something about this iconic Mexican bread.

MAKES ABOUT 10 ROLLS

500 g (1 lb 2 oz/3½ cups)
  bread flour
30 g (1 oz/2½ tablespoons) sugar
2 teaspoons active yeast
40 ml (1¼ fl oz/3 tablespoons) milk,
  at room temperature
250 ml (8½ fl oz/1 cup) warm water
25 ml (1 oz/2½ tablespoons)
  olive oil
1 teaspoon salt

1. In a large bowl, mix together the bread flour, sugar and yeast until well blended.

2. In a jug (pitcher), combine the milk, water and olive oil. Stir the liquid into the flour mixture, mixing with your hand until the dough forms a ball. Leave to sit for 5 minutes, covered, to let the flour absorb all the liquid. Add the salt, then knead for 10 minutes, until the dough is soft and elastic. If you are using a mixer with a dough attachment, mix on low speed for 6 minutes.

3. Place the dough in a lightly oiled bowl, cover with cling film (plastic wrap) and leave to rest until doubled in size. This should take 1–2 hours, depending on the temperature of the room.

4. Divide the dough into 10 equal pieces (about 75 g/2½ oz each). Press each piece of dough with the palm of your hand and gather the edges towards the centre to form a small ball. Turn the ball around and move it inside your hand in a circular motion while applying a bit of pressure. Place the rolled-up balls, round side-up, on a baking tray (pan) lined with baking parchment. Cover and leave for 15 minutes.

5. To form the *telera* breads, flatten each ball with the palm of your hand, then use a rolling pin, applying light pressure, to roll into a 12-cm (4¾-in) long oval shape. Rotate the dough so that it is landscape to you. Press the thicker end of a chopstick, or a thin spatula handle, lengthways along the dough, about a third of the way down. Press it hard enough to mark a line. Mark a second line, parallel to the first one, about two-thirds of the way down. You will have 2 lines running down the length of the oval shape.

6. Return the rolls to the lined tray, cover and leave to proof for about 40 minutes, until they double in size.

7. Meanwhile, preheat the oven to 190°C/170°C fan/375°F/gas mark 5. Bake the *telera* buns for 15–20 minutes, until golden and puffed.

Arroz a la Mexicana

In Mexican cooking, the term *a la Mexicana* refers to a dish with the colours of Mexican flag: the primary colours being green and red. *Arroz a la Mexicana* is an iconic dish that is on the table at every meal: colourful, fragrant red rice, with chopped carrots and peas traditionally mixed in or just decorated on top. I like this rice with sweetcorn kernels in addition to peas and carrots, and sometimes even potatoes are added.

SERVES 4

250 g (9 oz/1¼ cups) basmati rice
4 tablespoons vegetable oil
2 garlic cloves, peeled and crushed
250 g (9 oz) *Caldillo de Jitomate* (page 51)
½ teaspoon salt
about 250 ml (8½ fl oz/1 cup) Vegetable Stock (page 72)
60 g (2 oz) carrot, diced and blanched
60 g (2 oz) peas, blanched
60 g (2 oz) sweetcorn kernels, blanched

1. Rinse the rice several times until the water runs clear. Drain well and set aside.

2. Heat the oil in a large saucepan over a low heat, then add the garlic and fry for 1 minute, or until lightly coloured, being careful that it does not burn or turn too dark. Add the rice and fry for a couple of minutes until slightly translucent, stirring all the time. You want all the grains to be coated with oil.

3. Add the *Caldillo de Jitomate* and bring the mixture to the boil. Add the salt and 200 ml (7 fl oz/scant 1 cup) of the vegetable stock. Simmer for about 20 minutes, covered, checking occasionally. If it looks like it needs more stock, add a little more. Five minutes before the end of the cooking time, add the vegetables.

4. When all the liquid has been absorbed and the rice is cooked, turn off the heat and leave, covered, for 5 minutes. Fluff with a fork and serve.

Totopos

Totopos are usually made from fried tortillas, but I prefer to bake them for a healthier alternative. You can use the recipe for tortillas (page 57) or use good-quality store-bought tortillas. Serve the *totopos* with your favourite salsa or dipped in *Queso Fundido* (page 181), or as *chilaquiles*, tossed in your choice of salsa *verde*, salsa *roja* or even *mole*.

MAKES ABOUT 300 G (10 OZ)

16 tortillas (12 cm/4½ in or 15 cm /6 in in diameter)
2–3 tablespoons grapeseed or vegetable oil
fine sea salt

1. Preheat the oven to 170°C/150°C fan/340°F/gas mark 3½ and line a baking tray (pan) with baking parchment.

2. Lightly brush the tortillas with the oil and sprinkle them with sea salt. Cut each one into quarters using a sharp knife and spread out the pieces on the prepared baking tray.

3. Bake for 20–25 minutes, turning half way through. Turn off the oven, leaving the door slightly ajar to let the steam escape. Leave the *totopos* to cool and crisp up in the oven for 30 minutes.

Crema

As a child, one of my fondest memories of visiting *tianguis* (what we would now call a farmers' market) with my mum or grandma is getting a tostada as a reward once all the shopping was done, with a smear of cream and a sprinkle of *queso fresco*. Mexican *crema* is very lightly sour. This recipe is easy to make and is the closest thing to the authentic taste. It's perfect for adding to tacos or *tostadas*, or you can simply cook with it.

MAKES 600 G (1 LB 5 OZ)

500 ml (17 fl oz/2 cups) double (heavy) cream
125 ml (4 fl oz/½ cup) buttermilk

1. Place the cream and buttermilk in a non-reactive bowl and mix until well blended. Place the bowl over a saucepan of simmering water and stir until the mixture reaches about 37°C (98°F), the same temperature as your body.

2. Cover with cling film (plastic wrap) and leave at room temperature overnight. The mixture will have thickened and acquired a very light sour taste. It will keep well in the refrigerator for up to 1 week.

Queso Fresco

Queso fresco is a crumbly white cheese with a mild flavour. It softens the heat of chillies or salsas and adds melt-in-the-mouth creaminess. We use it sprinkled on many dishes, and it is a key ingredient for many *antojitos Mexicanos*, like *sopes*, *huaraches*, *flautas*, *tostadas*, etc. When making *queso fresco*, all your utensils and bowls need to be scrupulously cleaned and rinsed with boiling water. You don't want the wrong bacteria to spoil your cheese. Wrapping the *queso fresco* in dried avocado leaves gives it a wonderfully subtle aniseed aroma and flavour.

This recipe was originally shared with me by Kristen Schnepp, who ran a very successful dairy business under the arches in Peckham, London, for several years, selling a selection of Chihuahua, Oaxaca and, of course, *fresco* cheeses.

MAKES ABOUT 350 G (12 OZ)

2 litres (70 fl oz/8 cups) unhomogenised full-fat milk
4 tablespoons lime juice
¼ teaspoon vegetarian rennet
½ teaspoon non-iodised salt flakes
8 dried avocado leaves, softened in warm water for 10 minutes

1. Pour half the milk into a large bowl. Add the lime juice and stir, then leave to curdle for 15 minutes.

2. Fill a medium-sized saucepan with water and bring to the boil, then lower the heat to a gentle simmer. Remove ½ teaspoon of the boiled water and set it aside in a small cup to cool.

3. In a large heatproof bowl, combine the curdled milk with the rest of the milk. Set the bowl on top of the pan of simmering water to create a bain-marie. The bottom of the bowl should not touch the water.

4. Gently heat the milk mixture until it reaches 40°C (104°F) on a digital thermometer (this should take 20–25 minutes), then remove the bowl from the heat.

5. Stir the rennet into the teaspoon of cooled boiled water, then pour this mixture into the warm milk. Gently stir for 20 seconds to incorporate the rennet. The mixture will curdle. Cover the bowl with cling film (plastic wrap) and leave for 1 hour to set.

6. After an hour, bring the pan of water back to a simmer. Remove the cling film from the bowl and place it back on top of the simmering water. Check the temperature every 3 minutes. When it reaches 40°C (104°F), which should only take about 10 minutes, keep it at that temperature for 15 minutes, removing the pan from the heat if it gets too hot. The heat will firm up the curds.

7. Ladle the curds into a muslin cloth set over a sieve (fine mesh strainer). Twist and gently squeeze, then gather together the ends of the muslin, tie in a knot and hang from the tap to drain. Leave hanging for 45 minutes.

8. When ready, place the muslin bundle in a bowl. Open the muslin and mix the salt into the curds. The salt will draw more moisture out of the cheese. Re-tie the bundle and hang the cheese for another 30 minutes.

9. Your *queso fresco* is now ready. Sandwich it between two layers of avocado leaves and wrap in cling film. It will keep refrigerated for 1 week. After this time, it will still be good, but will taste stronger.

Black Beans with Avocado Leaves

Beans and *Arroz a la Mexicana* (page 64) are the classic accompaniments to the majority of *guisados* served in Mexican households. The secret to cooking beans is to cook them at a rolling boil for the first 10 minutes to remove any impurities that rise to the surface, then a bare simmer for at least 2 hours. I use dried avocado leaves: like kombu, they help make the beans easier to digest. The leaves can be toasted for a few seconds on each side to enhance their aniseed flavour. A blended version of these black beans can be turned into Avocado Black Bean *Refritos* (page 71).

MAKES 1.8 KG (3 LB 15 OZ)

500 g (1 lb 2 oz) dried black beans
2.2 litres (74 fl oz/ 8¾ cups) water
6–8 dried avocado leaves,
    depending on the size
1 onion, quartered
4 garlic cloves, peeled
2 tablespoons vegetable oil
10 g (½ oz/2 teaspoons) fine
    sea salt

1. Soak the black beans in water overnight. The next morning, wash and drain them twice.

2. To cook the beans, place them in a large cooking pot or saucepan. Cover with the 2.5 litres (85 fl oz/10 cups) cold water and bring to the boil. Boil for 10 minutes, removing the white foam that forms on the surface.

3. Meanwhile, dry-toast the avocado leaves in a frying pan (skillet) over a medium heat for 10 seconds on each side.

4. In a food processor, blend together the onion quarters, garlic cloves and oil. Add this mixture to the beans, along with the avocado leaves. Reduce the heat to a bare simmer and cook for at least 2 hours – but ideally longer – until the beans are soft and the liquid becomes thick. Stir the beans often so they don't catch at the bottom of the pot. If the beans become dry, add extra water during the cooking process and adjust the seasoning accordingly. Add the fine sea salt at the end and taste to check seasoning and balance.

5. Remove the avocado leaves and leave to cool.

Pinto Beans

About 70 different types of bean are grown in Mexico. Depending on the region, the altitude or the minerals in the soil, the beans acquire different speckles and deeper, richer colours. Black beans and pinto beans remain the most commonly exported. Pinto beans, or *frijol pinto*, meaning 'speckled beans' are used for refried beans because of their creamy texture. Mexicans cook their beans in a pressure cooker, which reduces the cooking time from about 2–3 hours to just 30 minutes.

MAKES 1.8 KG (3 LB 15 OZ)

500 g (1 lb 2 oz) pinto beans
2.5 litres (85 fl oz/10 cups) water
1 onion, quartered
4 garlic cloves, peeled
2 tablespoons grapeseed or
 vegetable oil
6 large bay leaves
10 g (¼ oz/2 teaspoons) fine
 sea salt

1. Soak the beans in a large bowl of water overnight. The next morning, wash and drain them twice.

2. Place the drained beans in a large cooking pot. Cover with the 2.5 litres (85 fl oz/10 cups) cold water, then place over a high heat and bring to the boil. Boil for 10 minutes, skimming off any white foam that forms on the surface.

3. Meanwhile, place the onion quarters, garlic cloves and oil in a food processor and blend until smooth. Add the mixture to the beans, along with the bay leaves. Reduce the heat to a bare simmer and cook for at least 2 hours – but ideally longer – until the beans are soft and the liquid becomes thick. Pinto beans absorb more water than black beans, so add a bit more water during cooking if needed. Stir often, making sure nothing catches at the bottom of the pan. Add the salt at the end and taste to check the seasoning. Leave to cool, and remove the bay leaves.

4. The beans will keep in the refrigerator for up to 1 week and in the freezer for 6 months.

NOTE: The recipe as it is works well for soupy Pinto Beans freshly cooked but they can also be reduced and refried with *Mojo de Ajo* (page 49) for an alternative and vegetarian take on refried beans, and topped with fresh *Pico de Gallo* (page 133) and *Queso Fresco* (page 67) as a serving suggestion.

Refried Beans

One of my earliest memories of eating delicious refried beans was in the state of Puebla, near Atlixco. I learned that the secret to proper refrying was good-quality fat (normally lard) with an optional touch of chilli – not for spiciness, but to add a delicate flavour and enhance the taste. Remember, I was a serious eater from the age of five!

Refried beans taste much better if they are freshly made, so keep a regular supply of cooked pinto beans and refry them as you need them.

MAKES 800 G (1 LB 12 OZ)/SERVES 4

½ quantity Pinto Beans (see left)
25 g (1 oz) goose fat
1 teaspoon Guajillo *Adobo* (page 89)
¼ teaspoon sea salt

1. Place half of the beans and some of their juices in a food processor. Blend until smooth, adding more cooking juices if needed, until the mixture has the consistency of a loose paste.

2. Place a frying pan (skillet) over a medium heat and add the goose fat. Once it's hot, add the guajillo *adobo* and mix well for a few seconds. Stir in the bean paste, along with the rest of the pinto beans, and fry for about 10 minutes, stirring constantly with a wooden spoon. I like my refried beans with some texture, which is why I leave some of the beans whole. The constant stirring mashes them as they reduce, and they absorb the flavour from the guajillo and goose fat.

3. Add the salt and enjoy straight away, topped with some crumbled *Queso Fresco* (page 67) and served with *Totopos* (page 65). Simplicity at its best.

Avocado Black Bean *Refritos*

I love to lightly fry black beans in a little *Mojo de Ajo*, adding Chipotle *en Adobo* purée. This enhances the flavour and adds an extra layer of smokiness and spice. You can use these black beans as a dip, a topping for *tostadas* or in the *Molletes* with *Pico de Gallo* (page 133).

MAKES 900 G (2 LB)

½ quantity Black Beans with Avocado Leaves (page 68)
30 g (1 oz) *Mojo de Ajo* (page 49)
20 g (¾ oz) Chipotle *en Adobo* Purée (page 82)
¼ teaspoon sea salt

1. Place the beans and some of their juices in a food processor. Blend until smooth, adding some more cooking juices if needed. You want the consistency to be that of a loose paste.

2. Heat the *Mojo de Ajo* in a frying pan (skillet) until hot. Add the bean paste and fry for 10 minutes, stirring occasionally. Add the chipotle paste and mix well, then season.

3. Use straight away or leave to cool. It will keep in the refrigerator for up to 5 days.

Chicken Stock

**MAKES 1.7 LITRES
(60 FL OZ/6¾ CUPS)**

1 chicken
2.5 litres (85 fl oz/10 cups)
   cold water
2 onions, halved
1 head of garlic, skin on, halved
3-cm (1¼-in) piece of fresh ginger
   root, peeled and sliced
200 g (7 oz) carrots, scrubbed and
   roughly chopped
3 bay leaves
3 sprigs of thyme
15 g (½ oz) coriander (cilantro)
¾ teaspoon salt

1. Place the chicken in a pot big enough to fit it snugly and cover with the water. Place over a low to medium heat and slowly bring to a simmer, removing any white foam as it rises to the surface.

2. Add the rest of the ingredients and simmer gently for 1 hour, turning the chicken over half way through. Remove the chicken from the stock and set aside, covered, to cool (see Tip).

3. Increase the heat to high for 20–30 minutes to reduce the stock and concentrate the flavours. Strain and set aside until ready to use. The stock will keep in the refrigerator for up to 4 days, or in the freezer for up to 6 months.

TIP: Once the chicken is cool enough to handle, shred the meat off the bone. You can use it in a recipe straight away, or it will keep in the refrigerator for up to 3 days.

Vegetable Stock

**MAKES 800 ML
(28 FL OZ/3¼ CUPS)**

2 onions, halved
1 head of garlic, skin on, halved
3-cm (1¼-in) piece of fresh ginger
   root, peeled and sliced
200 g (7 oz) carrots, scrubbed and
   roughly chopped
3 bay leaves
3 sprigs of thyme
15 g (½ oz) coriander (cilantro)
½ teaspoon salt
1.5 litres (53 fl oz/6 cups) water

1. Place all the ingredients in a 2-litre (70-fl oz) pot and place over a medium to high heat. Bring to the boil, then reduce the heat to medium to low and simmer for 45 minutes.

2. Strain the stock and set aside until ready to use. It will keep in the refrigerator for up to 4 days or in the freezer for up to 6 months.

Smoked Ham Hock

I prefer the taste of smoked ham in my recipes, but if you don't, you can just use an unsmoked ham hock. If that's the case, you should also use regular garlic cloves rather than smoked.

**MAKES 400 G
(14 OZ)**

1 x 1 kg (2 lb 3 oz) smoked ham hock
½ onion
3 smoked garlic cloves
5 morita chillies
3 bay leaves

1. Place the ham hock in a large bowl or pot of water and leave to soak for at least 3 hours. You should change the water twice during this soaking time.

2. Remove the ham from its soaking water, then rinse under the tap and place in a large pot. Cover with cold water, making sure the hock is completely submerged. Place the pot over a high heat and bring to the boil, removing any froth that forms on the surface.

3. Reduce the heat to medium low, add the rest of the ingredients and simmer very gently for about 2 hours, until the meat is tender and detaches easily from the bones.

4. Take off the heat and leave the ham to cool in its cooking liquid. Once it is cool enough to handle, but still warm, remove it from the pot. Remove the skin and fat and shred the meat off the bone. If you like, you can use it straight away, but if you want to store it, place it in an airtight container with a bit of the stock to keep it moist. Store in the refrigerator for up to 1 week, or freeze for up to 6 months.

MARINADES, RUBS AND SALSAS

Marinados, Adobos y Salsas

Chillies are one of the fundamental pillars of Mexican food. They are there to accentuate the flavours of a dish. They should not overpower the other individual elements, whether those are herbs, spices vegetables or a wonderful piece of meat or seafood. These salsas, rubs and marinades use some of my favourite chillies. I have used them in a variety of ways and have combined them with a whole host of ingredients I love that are native to England. These include jalapeño mayonnaise for crab *tostadas* made with freshly caught crab in Cornwall and the *Barbacoa Adobo* for cooking venison I source from the wonderful family-run West Country farm, whose produce is among my favourite in the UK. These salsas are used in the recipes throughout this book, but I encourage you to use them with a whole array of meats, fish and vegetables. Whether you drizzle Salsa *Macha* over your eggs on toast or add Beetroot and Pasilla Mixe Ketchup to a homemade burger, these flavours will bring a taste of Mexico to any dish.

Salsa *Roja Cruda*, Salsa *Roja Cocida*

This is a great example of the infinite variety of salsas in Mexican cooking. Different flavours and textures can be achieved from one basic salsa recipe. *Crudo* or *cruda* means something that has not been cooked, and it is also slang for being hungover: '*Estoy bien crudo*' means 'I'm extremely hungover'.

Salsa *roja cruda* pairs raw tomatoes with other raw ingredients like garlic, onion, chilli and fresh herbs. Only slightly spicy, salsa *cruda* is essentially a liquid salad. It is usually served with fried *antojitos Mexicanos*, such as tacos *dorados*, *flautas* or *pescadillas*.

Salsa *roja cocida* (meaning cooked) is traditionally prepared by charring all the ingredients. The smokiness of red onion, garlic and chilli roasted in a *comal* pairs perfectly with the charred tomato. I have also included a quicker version of the salsa that is not charred.

Salsa *de habanero de molcajete* is a hotter version of salsa *roja*, made with habanero chillies. You can use a food processor for the recipes below for convenience, which I think works well for the salsa *cruda*, but when the ingredients are roasted, I prefer crushing them in a *molcajete*, the Mexican mortar. The *molcajete* and its pestle, called the *tejolote* or, more commonly, *mano*, are carved from the volcanic formation of basalt. The grain of this rock produces a unique texture.

However you choose to prepare them, these salsas are delicious with *totopos* or as an accompaniment for *antojitos*.

MAKES ABOUT 480 G (1 LB 1 OZ)

1 red onion, quartered
4 garlic cloves
1 serrano or jalapeño chilli
5 ripe tomatoes, roughly chopped
½ teaspoon salt
juice of ¼ lime
5 g (¼ oz) coriander (cilantro) leaves, chopped

For salsa *roja cruda*

Place all the ingredients except the lime and coriander in a blender or food processor and blend until the mixture has the smooth texture of a runny salsa. Add a little water if needed. For a chunkier salsa, pulse three to four times instead of blending. Transfer to a bowl and stir in the lime and coriander. Taste and adjust seasoning if needed.

For salsa *roja cocida*

I like it best when all the ingredients are charred or roasted. Place the tomatoes, onion, garlic and chilli in a in a *comal* or a non-stick heavy frying pan over a medium heat and roast for 20 minutes until charred and soft. Make sure they are fully cooked, but keep an eye on them, as they might char at different speeds depending on their size. Alternatively, you can roast the vegetables in an oven preheated to 200°C/180°C fan/400°F/gas mark 6 for 30-40 minutes. They will not char as much, but they should still be roasted and soft. Remove from the *comal* or oven and allow to cool. Transfer all the ingredients to a *molcajete* (or food processor) and crush (or process) until you achieve the desired runny texture (adding water if needed). Transfer to a bowl and stir in the lime and coriander. Taste and adjust seasoning if needed.

To turn salsa *roja cruda* into a quick salsa *roja cocida*

If your plan is to turn this salsa *cruda* into salsa *roja cocina*, I would recommend adding the coriander at the very end when the salsa is cooling – this will prevent it from cooking and turning black. Heat 2 tablespoons of vegetable oil in a frying pan (skillet). Pour in the salsa *roja cruda* and cook for a few minutes until the colour changes to a deeper red. Don't let it reduce too much. This makes a great quick salsa for *chilaquiles*.

NOTE: If you purchase a brand new *molcajete*, it will need to be cured to avoid any basalt grit in your salsas. The process is easy: just grind a small handful of rice until it turns into a powder, making sure you crush it all over the inside of the *molcajete*. Repeat the process a few times until the mortar is smooth and any cracks are filled. Over time, the garlic, chillies and spices you use it to crush will also season the *molcajete* and therefore the food you prepare in it.

Habanero and Pumpkin Seed Salsa *Macha*

Salsa *macha* is traditionally a sauce made with oil, dried chillies and nuts (usually peanuts). Cooks in Mexico are inventive, so there are plenty of variations, but all versions give importance to the chilli and the varying textures and flavours of roasted nuts, seeds and spices. Salsa *macha* can be used as a salad dressing, and is also delicious drizzled on raw or grilled fish, meat or vegetables. I like the flavour and the heat of dried habanero chillies in this spicy version, which is also a base for my *Sikil Pak* Dip (page 98).

MAKES ABOUT 160 G (6 OZ)

40 g (1½ oz/¼ cup) pumpkin seeds
10 g (½ oz/1 tablespoon) sesame seeds
1 tablespoon balsamic vinegar
1 tablespoon *Mojo de Ajo* (page 49)
½ teaspoon salt
1 tablespoon lime juice
2 tablespoons orange juice
6 dried habanero chillies, ground to a powder
60 ml (2 fl oz/¼ cup) extra virgin olive oil

1. Dry toast the pumpkin seeds in a small frying pan (skillet) over a low-medium heat for a couple of minutes until they start to pop and are slightly toasted. Set aside to cool. Using the same pan, toast the sesame seeds for a few minutes until golden, then set aside to cool.

2. In a bowl, mix together the balsamic vinegar, *Mojo de Ajo*, salt and lime and orange juice until well blended. Gradually whisk in the oil, then incorporate the pumpkin seeds, habanero chilli powder and sesame seeds.

3. The salsa will keep in a glass container in the refrigerator for a couple of weeks. Eat at room temperature.

Salsa *Roja* de Molcajete

Dried or smoked chillies, like ancho or chipotle (and its variations, like meco or morita), also work well in this sauce, as do guajillo chillies. I encourage you to try all different kinds until you find your favourite combination. If you are using dried chillies, toast them in a *comal* or a non-stick heavy frying pan (skillet) until they are soft and pliable. Press on the chillies with a spatula as they cook and turn them often to distribute the heat. Be careful not to burn them – this would give a bitter flavour to the salsa or *adobo*. Place the toasted chillies in a bowl, cover with water, and leave to soak for at least 1 hour to rehydrate properly and softened before combining with the rest of the ingredients and turning into salsa.

MAKES ABOUT 350 G (12 OZ)

4 ripe plum tomatoes
1 red onion, quartered
4 garlic cloves
2–3 jalapeño chillies
½ teaspoon salt
5 g (¼ oz) coriander (cilantro) leaves, chopped
juice of ½ lime

1. Place the tomatoes, onion, garlic and chillies in a *comal* or a heavy non-stick frying pan (skillet) over a medium to high heat and roast for 25–30 minutes until charred and soft. Alternatively, you can roast the vegetables in an oven preheated to 200°C/180°C fan/400°F/gas mark 6 for 40 minutes. They will not char as much, but they should still be roasted and soft.

2. Remove from the *comal* (or oven) and allow to cool. Once cooled, put all these ingredients into your *molcajete* (or, alternatively, a food processor) and crush (or process), until you achieve a runny and smooth but still chunky texture – you can add a bit of water if needed. Season with the salt, add the coriander and lime juice and mix well with a spatula or spoon.

3. Serve with *Totopos* (page 65) or as an accompaniment for tacos.

Salsa *de habanero de molcajete*

To make salsa *de habanero de molcajete*, a hotter version of salsa *roja*, substitute the jalapeño chillies for 1–2 fresh habanero chillies.

Homemade Chipotles *en Adobo*

Chipotle chillies are made from ripe red jalapeño chillies. They are dried in the sun and lightly smoked. You can find different varieties – here, I'm using morita chipotle chillies, a mildly smoked chipotle, but I must admit that *meco* chillies are my favourite because of the intensity of their smokiness. However, either one will work well here. *Piloncillo* is essentially Mexican raw cane sugar, but if you cannot find it, you can use brown sugar or muscovado.

**MAKES 865 G
(1 LB 14½ OZ)**

700 ml (24 fl oz/scant 3 cups) water
100 g (3½ oz) dried morita
  chipotle chillies
3 bay leaves
150 g (5 oz) Onion *Sofrito* (page 50)
150 ml (5 fl oz/scant ⅔ cup) raw
  cider vinegar
4 smoked garlic cloves, peeled
4 black garlic cloves, peeled
70 g (2½ oz/1/3 cup) piloncillo or
  brown/muscovado sugar
15 g (½ oz/4 teaspoons) sea salt
1 tablespoon balsamic vinegar, plus
  1 tablespoon extra if you are
  making the purée

1. Bring the water to the boil in a medium-sized saucepan over a high heat. Drop in the morita chillies and bay leaves, then reduce the heat to very low and simmer for about 10 minutes until the chillies are soft and the liquid has reduced by a third.

2. Add the Onion *Sofrito*, cider vinegar, smoked and black garlic, brown sugar or piloncillo and sea salt, and continue to simmer for about 20 minutes until thickened and reduced. Stir the mixture often so that nothing sticks to the bottom of the pan. The chillies, garlic and onions should be falling apart, melting into a fragrant and unctuous sauce. Reduce the heat to low if needed. Taste, and adjust the seasoning by adding a little more salt or sugar to balance the flavours.

3. Remove from the heat. Once the mixture has cooled, remove the bay leaves and stir in the balsamic vinegar.

To make chipotle *en adobo* purée

Use a hand-held blender to blend half of the above mixture with an additional 1 tablespoon balsamic vinegar until smooth. This purée is a must-have ingredient to add to everything from *guisados* (stews) to quick salsas, or to smear on *tortas*. It will keep in the refrigerator for up to 1 month.

Ancho Dry Rub

This is a grown-up version of a slightly sweet chilli powder called *miguelito*. It is eaten as a candy, but also sprinkled over mango, jicama, cucumber or popcorn by street vendors. A special treat, especially after school! To make a powder for rubs or marinades, dried chillies are toasted, then ground. You can use your *molcajete* (page 78) – or a coffee grinder, for a less authentic (although much quicker) alternative!

I like using ancho chilli in this recipe, which is the dried version of much loved poblano peppers (pictured). It adds the fruitiness and the sweetness of a sundried tomato or raisin to this rub with a mild spice note.

**MAKES ABOUT 80 G
(3 OZ)**

30 g (1 oz) dried ancho chillies, trimmed
2 teaspoons fennel seeds
1 teaspoon coriander seeds
½ teaspoon ground cinnamon
1½ teaspoons salt
1½ teaspoons soft brown sugar
juice of 1 orange (optional)

1. Toast the chillies in a *comal* or non-stick frying pan (skillet) over a medium to high heat for a couple of minutes until soft and pliable. Be careful not to burn them or they will become bitter. Set aside to cool. Toast the fennel and coriander seeds in a small frying pan over a medium heat for a couple of minutes, until fragrant, then leave to cool.

2. Place the toasted chillies, fennel and coriander seeds, cinnamon, salt and sugar in a *molcajete* (or coffee grinder) and crush until finely ground. Transfer the mixture to a small bowl. Taste and adjust seasoning.

3. To use this as a seasoning, simply sprinkle it on fruit or vegetables, such as fresh pineapple, apples, cucumber or jicama. It's also great on popcorn.

4. To use it as a marinade or rub, add the orange juice and mix to create a thick paste. Rub it on chicken, pork, portobello mushrooms or even squash before roasting.

Barbacoa Adobo

Mexicans have made marinades into an art form. This *barbacoa adobo* perfectly balances the smokiness of chipotle chillies with the sweetness of ancho and the chocolate notes of pasilla mixe. It also incorporates dried avocado leaves, which bring a wonderful aniseed flavour. This marinade is used for the Lamb Shanks, *Barbacoa*-style on page 237, but it can also be used for barbecued chicken or vegetarian dishes, like the Smoky Cauliflower with *Mole Blanco* (page 238). Please note that the dried chillies require a 12-hour soak before use.

**MAKES 700 G
(1 LB 9 OZ)**

50 g (2 oz) morita chipotle chillies
2 ancho chillies
2 pasilla mixe chillies
500 ml (17 fl oz/2 cups) hot water
100 g (3½ oz) garlic cloves, peeled
2 teaspoons sea salt
2 tablespoons balsamic vinegar
20 g (¾ oz/1 tablespoon) dark
   agave syrup
10 dried avocado leaves
250 ml (8½ fl oz/1 cup)
   grapeseed oil

1. Place all the dried chillies in a bowl and pour the hot water over the top. Leave to soak for at least 12 hours. Soaking doesn't just soften the chillies; it also helps temper their heat. Once they are soft, drain the chillies, reserving the soaking water. Remove and discard all stems.

2. Place the chillies in a blender or food processor, along with most of the soaking water and the garlic. Blend until smooth, then add the salt, balsamic vinegar, agave syrup and avocado leaves and blend again until the leaves have disintegrated into the mixture. The marinade should be pourable but not runny. Add some more of the soaking water to adjust the thickness if needed.

3. Running the blender or food processor at a low speed, slowly add the oil and blend until emulsified.

4. Taste the marinade, being careful as it is very hot. This marinade should be on the salty side, so adjust the seasoning accordingly. Once you are satisfied, transfer the marinade to an airtight container. It is ready to use straight away, and will keep in the refrigerator for up to 1 week.

Salsa *Verde Cruda* and Avocado Salsa

One of my favourite salsas is salsa *cruda*. It is literally a liquid salad made of raw ingredients – *crudo* being Spanish for 'raw'. By adding beautifully ripe avocadoes to this simple base, you get a perfect smooth avocado salsa. You can serve it with *totopos,* of course, but in my opinion this is a must for *tacos dorados*. When turning the salsa *cruda* into an avocado salsa, I prefer to make it a little spicier, as its creamy texture beautifully balances the spicy notes of the fresh chillies and the herbal notes of the coriander. If you want to add more chillies or herbs, please feel free to do so.

MAKES ABOUT 600 G (1 LB 5 OZ)

500 g (1 lb 2 oz) fresh tomatillos, husked and roughly chopped

80–110 g (3–3¾ oz) green serrano or jalapeño chillies, roughly chopped

8 spring onions (scallions), chopped

10 g (½ oz) peeled garlic

35 g (1¼ oz) coriander (cilantro)

50 ml (1¾ fl oz/3 tablespoons) lime juice

2½ teaspoons salt

100 ml (3½ fl oz/scant ½ cup) water

TO MAKE IT INTO AVOCADO SALSA

2–3 avocados, peeled, stoned and chopped

an additional 10 g (½ oz) coriander (cilantro)

1. To make the salsa *cruda*, place the tomatillos, chillies, spring onions, garlic, coriander, lime juice, salt and water in a blender and blend until completely smooth. You now have salsa *cruda*.

2. To turn the salsa *cruda* into avocado salsa, add the flesh of 2 avocados to the previous mixture, along with the extra coriander. Blend until smooth. If you prefer a creamier texture, more like a thick dip, add the third avocado and blend until you obtain the desired texture. Taste for seasoning and adjust if needed.

NOTE: This works well with the Lamb Shank *Barbacoa* (page 237) or Ox Tongue Tacos (page 162). They will keep in a glass container in the refrigerator for 4–5 days.

Salsa *Verde* Cocida

This salsa uses the same ingredients as the Salsa *Verde Cruda*. They are dry-roasted in a heavy cast-iron flat pan or a *comal*. You can use a heavy-based frying pan (skillet). Once the ingredients are all blackened and soft, they can be blended. You can use tinned tomatillos for this salsa, but don't roast them or they will turn into a mush. To eliminate that slight metallic taste from the tinned tomatillos, my secret is to add a little grated ginger and to intensely roast the onion, garlic and chillies.

MAKES ABOUT 600 G (1 LB 5 OZ)

500 g (1 lb 2 oz) fresh tomatillos, husked, or use drained tinned tomatillos if you can't get fresh
80–110 g (3–3¾ oz) green serrano or jalapeño chillies, left whole
8 spring onions (scallions), left whole
10 g (½ oz) peeled garlic
35 g (1¼ oz) coriander (cilantro)
20 ml (1½ tablespoons) lime juice
2½ teaspoons salt

1. Place a large, heavy-based frying pan (skillet) over a medium heat and add the fresh tomatillos (if using), along with the chillies, spring onions and garlic. Dry-roast for 20–30 minutes until blackened and soft. Once roasted, set aside for 10 minutes to cool.

2. Once cooled, place all the roasted vegetables in the blender, along with the coriander, lime and salt. If you're used tinned tomatillos instead of fresh, add them to the blender now. Blend the salsa to your preferred consistency – you can make it very smooth, or just pulse to keep some texture.

3. It will keep in a glass container in the refrigerator for 4–5 days.

Guajillo *Adobo*

The guajillo chilli is a long and thin medium-hot chilli, mainly used dried. Once cooked in this vibrantly red *adobo*, it can be used cold to add zing to salsas or warm to perk up the colour and flavour of pan-fried prawns (page 208) or a *Pambazo* (page 169).

MAKES ABOUT 360 G (12¾ OZ)

120 g (4 oz) guajillo chillies, deseeded and stem removed
100 g (3½ oz) *Cebolla Morada* (page 50), plus 60 ml (2 fl oz/4 tablespoons) pickled liquid
2 teaspoons salt
juice of 1 lime

1. Toast the chillies in a *comal* or a heavy non-stick frying pan (skillet) over a medium heat until they are soft and pliable. Press down on the chillies with a spatula as they cook, and turn them often to distribute the heat. Be careful not to burn them – this would give a bitter flavour to the *adobo*. Place the cooked chillies in a bowl and cover with 400 ml (13 fl oz/1½ cups) water. Leave to soak for at least 1 hour.

2. Place the soaked chillies in a blender with 100 ml (3½ fl oz/scant ½ cup) of their soaking liquid and the rest of the ingredients. Blend until very smooth: the consistency should be slightly thick, but pourable. Pass through a fine sieve (fine mesh strainer), then blend again until very smooth. Taste to check the seasoning and adjust accordingly. This *adobo* will keep in the refrigerator for up to 1 month.

Adobo Verde

This is a fresh and non-traditional herby dressing, which has tones of lime and chillies, and can be used as a marinade or an *adobo*. It goes very well with seabass: simply spread a few tablespoons of the sauce between two fillets of seabass before baking. Alternatively, try it drizzled over grilled prawns (shrimp) or grilled vegetables, like courgettes (zucchini) or mushrooms.

MAKES ABOUT 600 G (1 LB 5 OZ)

3 green jalapeño chillies, trimmed, deseeded and very finely chopped

5 g (¼ oz) tarragon leaves, very finely chopped

30 g (1 oz) flat-leaf parsley, very finely chopped

5 spring onions (scallions), very finely chopped

30 g (1 oz) green olives, pitted and very finely chopped

2 teaspoons Mexican oregano

1 teaspoon salt

1 teaspoon freshly ground black pepper

100 ml (3½ fl oz/scant ½ cup) hemp oil

300 ml (10 fl oz/1¼ cups) sesame oil

2 tablespoons lime juice

1. Place the chillies, tarragon, parsley, spring onions and olives in a bowl. Add the oregano, salt and pepper and stir to combine.

1. Gradually incorporate the two oils, whisking between each addition. Finish the sauce by adding the lime juice. Taste and adjust the seasoning.

Salsa *de* Árbol

The árbol chilli is a short, thin chilli cultivated in the central provinces of Mexico. Its twig-like appearance is the origin of its name, which means 'tree like'. It is one of the hotter varieties of chillies, and comes from the same family as cayenne pepper. You will feel the strength of its heat when you toast it; make sure your kitchen is well ventilated. When working with these strong and spicy chillies, it's always advisable to wear kitchen gloves to avoid any issues after touching them. Just washing your hands won't be enough – I learned this the hard way.

This is a spicy sauce. Add just a touch to soft or crispy tacos, like tacos *dorados*.

**MAKES ABOUT 400 G
(14 OZ)**

15 g (½ oz) árbol chillies, stems removed
20 g (¾ oz) garlic, peeled
1 onion, roughly chopped
1 teaspoon salt
500 ml (17 fl oz/2 cups) water
60 g (2 oz) *Mojo de Ajo* (page 49)
100 g (3½ oz) Guajillo *Adobo* (page 89)

1. Toast the chillies in a *comal* or heavy non-stick frying pan (skillet) over a medium heat for about 30 seconds until slightly darkened. Press down on the chillies with a spatula as they cook, and turn them often, taking care not to burn them.

2. Place the toasted chillies in a saucepan over a low heat with the garlic, chopped onion and salt. Cover with the water and simmer for 10 minutes. Leave to cool slightly, then transfer the contents of the saucepan to a blender and blend until smooth.

3. Return the empty saucepan to the heat, and add the *Mojo de Ajo*. Cook until it starts to sizzle, then add the blended mixture and cook for 5 minutes. Add the Guajillo *Adobo* and simmer for another 5 minutes. The sauce is now ready. It will keep in the refrigerator for up to 2 weeks.

Pineapple and Apricot *Chamoy*

This is an iconic chilli sauce, traditionally made with dried chillies, salt, sugar and fresh apricots, which apparently has its roots in Japan. It is a perfect balance of sweet, spicy and sour. If you've been to Mexico, you will have noticed plastic bottles of *chamoy* on every *chicharrones* cart or fruit stand. Sadly, commercially produced *chamoy* is full of artificial colouring and flavours, so I want to share a healthy alternative that can be enjoyed by everyone. It is delicious drizzled on apples, pears, mangos or pineapple, or served with carrot and cucumber sticks.

MAKES ABOUT 500 ML (17 FL OZ/2 CUPS)

about 150 ml (5 fl oz/scant ⅔ cup) Hibiscus Cordial (page 55)
100 g (3½ oz) fresh pineapple, peeled and cut into chunks
1 teaspoon salt
1 piquín, dry habanero or árbol chilli, trimmed
40 g (1½ oz) dried apricots
30 g (1 oz) pitted dried prunes
juice of ½ orange
fresh fruit or crudités, to serve

1. Place the ingredients in a blender and blend until smooth. Pass through a fine sieve (mesh strainer) and blend again, adding a bit of extra cordial if needed. The *chamoy* should have the consistency of a runny ketchup.

2. Taste and adjust the seasoning if needed. Transfer to a jar or bottle. It will keep in the refrigerator for 2 weeks.

TIP: You can replace the prunes with raisins and additional apricots.

Salsa Pasilla Mixe

Pasilla mixe chillies, thin, long and reddish black, are the dried version of the green chilaca chillies grown at high altitude in the Sierra Mixe, north-east of the state of Oaxaca. The composition of the soil and the location greatly influence the taste of these chillies. The technique used to achieve their intense smokiness is a well-guarded secret among the local communities. Pasilla mixe and chipotle meco (from Puebla) are my two favourite chillies in Mexican cooking. Use this salsa as a dip with *totopos*, in *tamales* and in breakfast burritos. I genuinely love the smokiness and I hope you do as well.

**MAKES 660 G
(1 LB 7 OZ)**

60 g (2 oz) pasilla mixe chillies, trimmed and deseeded
1 cinnamon stick
500 ml (17 fl oz/2 cups) water
1 onion, quartered
10 garlic cloves, peeled
1½ teaspoons salt
2 teaspoons dark agave syrup
10 g (¼ oz) coriander (cilantro), finely chopped

1. Toast the chillies in a *comal* or a heavy non-stick frying pan (skillet) over a medium heat until they are soft and pliable. Press down on the chillies with a spatula as they cook, and turn them often to distribute the heat. Be careful not to burn them – this would give a bitter flavour to the salsa. Add the cinnamon stick to the pan and lightly toast to enhance the flavour and aroma. Place the toasted chillies and cinnamon stick in a bowl and cover with the water. Leave to soak for at least 1 hour.

2. Meanwhile, place the onion and garlic cloves in a *comal* or a non-stick heavy frying pan over a medium to high heat and roast for 10–15 minutes until charred and soft.

3. Drain the soaked chillies, reserving 150 ml (5 fl oz/scant ⅔ cup) of the soaking liquid. Place the chillies in a blender, along with the roasted onion and garlic. Add the salt, agave and reserved soaking liquid, plus 100 ml (3½ fl oz/scant ½ cup) fresh water. Blend until smooth – the consistency should be slightly thick and pourable. Pass through a fine sieve (mesh strainer), then blend again until very smooth.

4. Add the coriander, then check the seasoning and adjust if needed. This salsa will keep refrigerated for up to 2 weeks.

Beetroot and Pasilla Mixe Ketchup

Mexico City offers fantastic *hamburguesas al carbón*. Our proximity with the US might be part of what makes this fast food so popular in practically every neighbourhood. Burger stands or carts cooking *al carbón* (on charcoal) rather than on a *plancha* (griddle) are my favourites. This ketchup is extremely easy to prepare. If you can't find pasilla mixe chillies, you can try it with chipotle meco, chipotle morita or even ancho or mulato chillies.

I also like to serve it as an alternative to tomatillo ketchup with my Duck *Carnitas* (page 218), as the smokiness of the beetroot and pasilla mixe chillies makes a change from the sharpness and freshness of tomatillo, jalapeno and mint.

MAKES ABOUT 700 G (1 LB 9 OZ)

1 pasilla mixe chilli
150 ml (5 fl oz/scant ⅔ cup) cider vinegar
200 ml (7 fl oz/scant 1 cup) water
½ cinnamon stick
300 g (10 oz) raw beetroot (beets), peeled and cubed
2 apples, peeled, cored and quartered
60 g (2 oz/¼ cup) honey
40 g (1½ oz/3 tablespoons) caster (superfine) sugar
100 g (3½ oz) raisins
¾ teaspoon salt

1. Place the chilli, cider vinegar, water and cinnamon in a medium-sized saucepan over a high heat. Bring to a boil, then add the beetroot cubes, cover and reduce the heat to low. Simmer for 35–45 minutes, or until the beetroot is cooked and most of the liquid has been absorbed. Take off the heat and allow to cool.

2. Transfer the cooked beetroot and cinnamon into a blender. Add the rest of the ingredients and blend until smooth, then pass through a sieve (fine mesh strainer).

3. Pour the mixture back into the saucepan and simmer for 20 minutes until slightly thickened. Once cool, It will keep in a glass container in the refrigerator for a week.

NOTE: I make my favourite *hamburguesa* by mixing good-quality beef mince (ground beef) with 1 tablespoon of this ketchup, along with some chopped garlic, finely chopped parsley, grated Parmesan, finely chopped *Chiles en Escabeche* (page 46), tomato purée (paste), freshly crushed black pepper and a pinch of salt. Barbecue these juicy patties and top with Chihuahua or mild Cheddar cheese and more ketchup for the full experience. Serve with extra *Chiles en Escabeche*, slices of tomato and onion, and a scoop of smashed avocado. Mexican burger-umami at its best.

Xni' Pek (Mayan-style Habanero Salsa)

This salsa's name translates literally from the Mayan as 'dog's runny nose', based on the fact that this chunky Yucatecan salsa has a real kick. I like to use four chillies and their seeds, but feel free to use fewer chillies and deseed them. This makes the perfect accompaniment for Pibil-style Pork Ribs (page 234) or the classic recipe *Cochinita Pubil*, a truly Yucatecan experience.

MAKES 400 G (14 OZ)

1 large red onion, finely chopped

2–4 habanero or Scotch bonnet chillies, finely chopped

50 g (2 oz) *Cebolla Morada* (page 52), plus 30 ml (2 tablespoons) of the pickling juice

100 ml (3½ fl oz/scant ½ cup) orange juice

¾ teaspoons sea salt

40 ml (1¼ fl oz/3 tablespoons) extra virgin olive oil

20 g (¾ oz) coriander (cilantro), chopped

1. Place the finely chopped red onion, chillies and *Cebolla Morada* in a bowl and add the pickling juice, orange juice and salt. Mix well until the salt has dissolved.

2. Whisk in the olive oil and leave the salsa to infuse for 10 minutes. Taste to check seasoning and balance and adjust accordingly with more juice or chillies if needed. This salsa should be spicy – very spicy! – but with a fragrant and citrusy flavour. Add the coriander just before serving.

Sikil Pak (Habanero and Pumpkin Seed Chunky Dip)

Sikil pak is a famous Yucatecan dip of Mayan origin. Traditionally it contains charred tomato that is mashed and mixed with the other ingredients. My version is made by blending one of my favourite salsas, the Habanero and Pumpkin Seed Salsa *Macha*, with fresh orange juice and roasted pumpkin seeds, but you can of course add charred tomato, if you wish. I like to mix in extra freshly toasted pumpkin seeds at the end for texture.

MAKES ABOUT 200 G (7 OZ)

50 g (2 oz) pumpkin seeds
120 g (4 oz) Habanero and Pumpkin Seed Salsa *Macha* (page 79)
juice of 1 orange

1. Dry roast the pumpkin seeds in a non-stick frying pan (skillet) over a low to medium heat for a couple of minutes, shaking the pan all the time. When they are slightly toasted and a few start to pop, transfer them into a bowl and set aside to cool.

2. Place half the pumpkin seeds in a *molcajete* (page 78) or a small food processor. Add the Habanero and Pumpkin Seed Salsa *Macha*. If you are using a *molcajete*, start crushing and mixing, gradually adding the orange juice. If you are using a small food processor, pulse a few times, adding the orange juice between pulses, and stop when you obtain a chunky dip, before it turns into a purée.

3. Just before serving, incorporate the rest of the pumpkin seeds into the dip. The seeds will absorb all the liquids, and if it sits for too long, the dip will lose its crunchiness, so do this right at the end.

4. Serve at once with some crudités or *Totopos* (page 65).

EARLY MORNING

Al despertar

What do you have early in the morning in Mexico? Well that depends on where you are going or where you are coming from. When I was on the youth national rowing team I trained at the Olympic rowing course, Cuemanco, built for the 1968 Olympics in the city. My early mornings would always consist of a *jugo verde* from Beto's juice stand made with fresh cactus, pineapple, orange juice and spirulina. The elixir would restore me after the intense and arduous training session which began at 6am every morning. But after a night out, you would find me with friends at a taco stand enjoying *barbacoa* tacos and *consommé* – the broth the meat was cooked in – with chilli, lime, coriander and onion. We were convinced, as I still am to this day, that those tacos before heading home would negate any possible hangover. Or at least make it less intense!

Early morning in Mexico is the time of day when the city comes to life: the street traders meticulously set up their stalls for the day ahead, and the hum of traffic starts to fill the streets in a city notorious for its gridlocked roads. People are busy heading across the vast city in their cars or on buses that include old VW camper vans called 'combis', while street vendors on bicycles blast out a whole array of music to keep the *Chilangos* going. Like a giant beast waking from its slumber, the city springs to life, and those starting the day need sufficient sustenance: the working day can often stretch late into the night, and the traffic means that commutes can easily take several hours hours each morning. Vendors can be see going from car to car in gridlocked traffic, offering snacks and drinks to commuters, as well as hopping on and off buses selling early morning drinks, fruit cocktails or jelly. Among the first stands to set up in the morning are the fruit and juice stands. Mexico's year-round warm climate means it is blessed with some of the most wonderful tropical fruits that are incredibly sweet and full of flavour, including pineapples, papaya and mangos, as well as lesser-known fruits like mamey, dragon fruit and prickly pears. These are sold as fruit platters, in freshly pressed juices or smoothies and are a must as part of any early morning in Mexico. This is just a stop-gap before breakfast, which in Mexico is a big affair!

Hibiscus Infusion

Hibiscus juice is high in vitamins, making it a perfect way to start the day and fight winter colds. The dried flowers will keep well in the cupboard, and will therefore always be available. The hibiscus syrup used for the Hibiscus *Tamales* (page 124) is high in sugar. This is a similar recipe, but instead of sugar, you can use agave syrup to sweeten the drink to your liking.

MAKES 1 LITRE (34 FL OZ/4 CUPS)
70 g (2½ oz) hibiscus flowers
1 litre (34 fl oz/4 cups) water
dark agave syrup, to taste

1. Carefully wash the flowers under running water to remove any sand, stones or dirt stuck between the petals.

2. In a medium-sized saucepan, bring the water to the boil. Add the flowers, then stir constantly for about 10–15 minutes, until the flowers are soft but still firm and have released all of their flavour and colour in the water.

3. Remove the flowers with a skimmer or slotted spoon and set aside to use in a hibiscus compote (page 55) or a savoury filling (page 176). When all the flowers have been removed, add the dark agave to taste and stir until dissolved.

4. Leave to cool, then bottle up and keep in the refrigerator for up to 2 weeks.

Jugo Verde de Nopal

Nopales are the young pads of the nopal or prickly pear cactus. It is very difficult to find them fresh outside of Mexico, but when I do, I cook them in a copper pot – this is key to reducing the sliminess of boiled cactus. You can enjoy them in salads however I enjoy the most drinking it raw. They are widely used in Mexican cooking. With its high content of fibre, protein, antioxidants, vitamins, and minerals *nopal* is highly praised for its health benefits.

To peel the pads, hold them at the base and, using the back of a knife, scrape off the spines and bristle on both sides. A fish scaler also works well. Trim around the edges with a knife, and cut into strips or squares.

SERVES 1
100 g (3½ oz) sliced fresh cactus paddle
120 g (4 oz) fresh pineapple, roughly chopped
100 ml (3½ fl oz/scant ½ cup) orange juice
100 ml (3½ fl oz/scant ½ cup) water
1 teaspoon honey
5 g (½ oz) flat-leaf parsley

1. Place all the ingredients in a blender and blend at high speed for a few minutes to eliminate the sliminess of the cactus. This really is key, otherwise the juice could turn very slimy. Taste and adjust the sweetness. Serve at once – this juice is best if prepared at the last minute.

Rice *Horchata*

Queen of Mexican *agua frescas*, *horchata* is the ideal thirst quencher on a hot summer day. It is simply made with rice that has been soaked overnight and blended with water, cinnamon and vanilla. I like it cold, of course, but I also enjoy it in my morning coffee for a really comforting feel as a substitute for cow's milk.

MAKES 1 LITRE (34 FL OZ/4 CUPS)
300 g (10 fl oz/1¼ cups) rice
4 tablespoons caster (superfine) sugar
1 teaspoon ground cinnamon
1 tablespoon vanilla extract

1. Rinse the rice under running water until it runs clear. Place the rinsed rice in a bowl and cover with hot water. Leave overnight.

2. The next day, drain the rice, then place half of it in a powerful blender, along with half of the sugar, cinnamon and vanilla. Add 500 ml (17 fl oz/2 cups) water and blend until all the rice is processed and the liquid is smooth. Transfer to a jug (pitcher) and repeat with the remaining rice, sugar, cinnamon and vanilla and another 500 ml (17 fl oz/2 cups) water. Combine both batches and serve.

Avocado Shake

Puffed amaranth is quick and easy to make – it's almost instant. I always have a batch of puffed amaranth ready to use in my cupboard. You will see that I often sprinkle it on salads and add it to breakfast dishes. Make this avocado shake at the last minute or the avocado will oxidise. It is nutritious and perfect to sustain you throughout the morning.

SERVES 2
1 ripe avocado, peeled, stoned and roughly chopped
200 ml (7 fl oz/¾ cup) orange juice
200 ml (7 fl oz/¾ cup) apple juice
20 g (¾ oz) puffed amaranth (page 147)
2 teaspoons dark agave syrup

1. Place all the ingredients in a blender and blend until smooth. Divide between two glasses and serve straight away.

Spicy *Chocolate de Agua*

From pre-Hispanic times, chocolate drink was considered 'God's drink', and something that only be enjoyed by the elite few in Mayan and Aztec cultures. Coming from the Nahuatl word *xocolātl*, it literally means 'bitter water', as it was prepared with roasted cacao and a few spices. Cacao is a super food – and a super plant – that provides a lot of nutrients and has medicinal properties.

I use a high-quality cocoa powder in this recipe, as it is easier to source, but traditionally we would use Mexican chocolate tablets, which have a high cocoa content and are spiced with cinnamon and sugar. What makes this hot chocolate special is its foamy top. In Mexico we use a *molinillo*, a specially turned and carved tool dedicated to creating that foam. You can also use a whisk – less traditional, but effective.

In my opinion, the best hot chocolate comes from Cardenal Restaurant in Mexico City, where it is prepared and foamed in front of you. Accompanied by a *concha*, it is the beginning or end of a lazy but successful breakfast for us Mexicans.

SERVES 2

500 ml (17 fl oz/2 cups) water
1 cinnamon stick
1 morita chipotle or ½ ancho or árbol chilli
40 g (1½ oz/scant ½ cup) organic high-quality cocoa powder (or chopped Mexican chocolate tablets, if you can get them)
55 g (2 oz/¼ cup) brown sugar (not needed if you are using Mexican chocolate tablets)

1. Place the water in a saucepan and add the cinnamon stick and chilli. Bring to the boil and leave to simmer for 5 minutes until the water gets a slight tint from the cinnamon stick. Reduce the heat to a bare simmer and add the cocoa powder and brown sugar or the chopped chocolate. Stir regularly until the chocolate has melted.

2. Hold the *molinillo* between the palms of your hand and roll in a back and forth motion between the palms of your hands to beat the hot chocolate and create a foamy top. Alternatively, use a whisk.

3. Serve immediately.

Tepache

Tepache is like a Mexican pineapple kombucha. It is made from the peel and flesh of a very ripe pineapple, fermented with brown sugar and flavoured with spices. Like all fermented drinks, it is a natural probiotic, and this is why I have included it as a healthy drink in the breakfast section. Its flavour – a sort of yeasty cider – makes it a tasty accompaniment to a meal and an interesting mixer for cocktails. You will find a recipe using it in the Sundown Drinks section (page 202).

**MAKES ABOUT 1 LITRE
(34 FL OZ/4 CUPS)**

500 g (1 lb 2 oz/2½ cups) Demerara
  (dark brown) sugar
250 g (9 oz/1¼ cups) dark
  muscovado sugar or *piloncillo*
500 ml (17 fl oz/2 cups)
  boiling water
2 cinnamon sticks
1 teaspoon allspice berries
1 teaspoon cloves
1 small ancho chilli, stem removed,
  torn into pieces
½ teaspoon salt flakes
¼ teaspoon black peppercorns
1 star anise
5-cm (2-in) piece of fresh
  ginger root
1 very ripe medium-sized pineapple
  (ideally organic)
500 ml (17 fl oz/2 cups) cold water

1. In a large jug (pitcher), combine the sugars and boiling water and stir until the sugars are dissolved. Add the cinnamon sticks, allspice berries, cloves, chilli, salt, peppercorns, star anise and ginger and pour the mixture into a 2-litre (68-fl oz) glass jar.

2. Square off the base of the pineapple, then, holding it by the leaves, cut straight down along the fibrous core. Discard the core, which would give the tepache a bitter taste. Cut the pineapple into chunks, peel and all, and add to the glass jar. Top up with the cold water and swirl the contents to mix together.

3. Cover the mouth of the jar with a couple of layers of muslin (cheesecloth). The mixture will start to ferment after 48 hours. Skim the foam that has formed on the top and leave to sit for another day. You can start using your *tepache* after that time. Ideally, the jar should be kept at 25°C (77°F).

Café de Olla Syrup

This is the most iconic coffee alternative found in *taquerias*, *fondas*, traditional *cenadurías* and markets in the capital. It takes its name from the *olla de barro* (clay pot) in which it is made. It is typically prepared by boiling water with coffee grains, orange peel, cinnamon and *piloncillo* (raw sugar cane). I like preparing the syrup in advance so it is ready when I want to add it to my morning coffee!

**MAKES ABOUT 500 ML
(17 FL OZ/2 CUPS)**

1 litre (34 fl oz/4 cups) water
3 cinnamon sticks
1 star anise
peel of 1 orange
400 g (14 oz/2 cups) brown sugar

1. In a large saucepan over a high heat, bring the water to the boil. Add cinnamon, anise and orange peel and reduce the heat to low. Simmer for 10–15 minutes until the water has been properly infused and the volume has reduced by half.

2. Add the brown sugar and stir until dissolved. Leave to simmer for a further 5 minutes until the mixture has the consistency of a light syrup.

3. Allow to cool, then pour into a bottle to store.

naranja
ZAPOTE
mango
y
FRESA

JUGOS
de:

NAR
TORO
ZANA

VAMPIRO
*
Betabel
Naranja
Piña
Zanana

Jug
naranja
ZAPOTE

BEBIDAS

Caldo de chapulín

BREAKFAST

Desayuno

The best breakfasts are served in Mexico. Long before going out for brunch became popular, Mexicans would go for the equivalent breakfasts for business meetings, to meet with friends or to see family at the weekends. Going out for breakfast is definitely a part of the social calendar for many in Mexico City, and it can be one of the hardest times of day to get a table in some of the best restaurants.

Mexican breakfasts are a culinary representation of our country, its diversity, microclimate and traditions. One of our weekly rituals when I was a child was going for breakfast to a English inspired restaurant called La Cochera del Bentley ('The Bentley Garage'). My parents and their friends would enjoy their famous eggs Benedict while Mexican hot chocolate and pancakes where a hit with the younger audience. A 1970s Bentley bonnet took centre stage at the entrance and the restaurant prided itself on being quintessentially British. Little did I know I would end up setting up the inverse, a Mexican restaurant in London.

On my visits back to the city, I often like to start the day at a street food stall for an *atole*, a thick, filling drink made with corn and often flavoured with fruits or chocolate. I accompany it with a *tamale*, a corn-dough parcel filled with chicken, pork or vegetables, served with a salsa, which will fill you up for several hours.

My absolute favourite everyday breakfast is *chilaquiles* – crispy corn tortilla chips, drenched in salsa and topped with cream, cheese and red onion. You can enjoy these everywhere from street stands or in the city's most iconic restaurants. In Mexico's picturesque Condesa neighbourhood, there is even a street corner known as *La Esquina del Chilaquil*. It's run by Perla Guzman, whose grandmother started selling food from that same corner over 70 years ago. Every day of the year Perla and her family get up at 4am to start to prepare the food and from 8am to 1pm serve a queue that can span the entire block. The options are simple, red or green *chilaquiles*, served with black beans, cream, cheese and chicken in breadcrumbs. The combination is sublime.

For a breakfast steeped in tradition El Cardenal, in the historic centre, has been serving Mexican cuisine with impeccable service since the 1960s. Back then it was the favoured breakfast spot of the country's top politicians. The white tablecloths, grandiose wooden staircase and smartly dressed servers will leave you feeling that you have gone back in time to an era of decadence and luxury. And the freshly baked pastries and Mexican hot chocolate provide a wonderful start to the day which are hard to beat.

French Toast with Agave, Cacao Nibs and Bacon

Cinnamon plays a big part in Mexican cooking. While these delicate quills are not indigenous to Mexico and were originally imported from Sri Lanka, states like Veracruz and Tabasco now produce cinnamon. What makes this French toast unique is its coating of cinnamon sugar. Use thick brioche slices to get the full contrast between the moist centre and crispy topping.

SERVES 4

300 ml (10 fl oz/1¼ cups) milk
2 large eggs
1 teaspoon vanilla extract
½ teaspoon ground cinnamon
8 rashers (slices) of smoked back
    or streaky bacon
4 tablespoons dark agave syrup
20 g (¾ oz/1½ tablespoons) butter
200 g (7 oz) stale brioche loaf, cut
    into thick slices

FOR THE COATING

1 tablespoon ground cinnamon
4 tablespoons caster (superfine)
    sugar

FOR THE TOPPING

60 g (2 oz) Granola with Amaranth
    (page 138)
15 g (½ oz) cacao nibs
1 tablespoon agave syrup, to drizzle

1. Preheat the oven to 200°C/180°C fan/400°F/gas mark 6 and line a baking tray (pan) with baking parchment.

2. Combine the milk, eggs, vanilla and cinnamon in a medium-sized bowl and whisk until well blended. Set aside.

3. Brush the bacon rashers on both sides with the agave syrup and place on the prepared baking tray. Bake for about 6 minutes on each side, or until well caramelised. Set aside and keep warm.

4. Melt the butter in a large frying pan (skillet) over a very low heat. Dip each brioche slice into the egg mixture, then place into the frying pan. Cook for 2 minutes on each side, or until golden.

5. Meanwhile, prepare the cinnamon sugar coating by mixing together the cinnamon and sugar in a small bowl and setting aside.

6. Transfer the brioche slices on to serving plates and lightly dust on both sides with the cinnamon sugar. Top with the bacon rashers, then sprinkle with the granola and cocoa nibs. Finish with a drizzle of agave syrup and serve.

Atole de Fresas

Corn is both eaten and drunk in Mexico! Traditionally, the fresh corn *masa* is diluted into water to thicken it, but here, I use dry *masa harina* and flavour it with fresh fruit purée, cinnamon and sugar. My kids love it with strawberries, which is what I've used here. *Atole* will give you all the strength you need to start your cold winter day. You can swap the strawberries for blackberries, or even Mexican chocolate tablets to turn this into a chocolate *atole*.

SERVES 4

800 ml (28 fl oz/3¼ cups) water
80 g (3 oz/¾ cup) dry *masa harina*
90 g (3¼ oz/½ cup) caster (superfine) sugar
½ teaspoon ground cinnamon
500 g (1 lb 2 oz) strawberries, hulled

1. In a medium-sized saucepan, bring 400 ml (13 fl oz) of the water to a simmer over a medium heat.

2. In a jug (pitcher), dilute the *masa harina* in 300 ml (10 fl oz/1¼ cups) cold water, then whisk this mixture into the simmering water. Add the sugar and cinnamon and simmer for 10–15 minutes, stirring occasionally, until the mixture thickens.

3. Place the strawberries in a blender with the remaining 100 ml (3½ fl oz/scant ½ cup) water and blend until smooth. If your blender is not powerful enough to crush the strawberry seeds, pass the mixture through a sieve (fine mesh strainer). Stir the strawberry purée into the mixture in the saucepan and simmer for another 5 minutes. Taste and adjust the sugar, then serve hot.

Chilaquiles Verde with Fried Eggs

This is one of the dishes that I enjoy the most. It combines the flavours and textures I love best in Mexican cooking, and can be found on breakfast, lunch and even dinner menus! I genuinely believe that there are no rules for *chilaquiles*, as long as *totopos* are kept crunchy and fully covered in salsa. My wife Natalie agrees, and her favourites are *chilaquiles verdes*. I also like *chilaquiles* with *mole*: just substitute the salsa *verde* for the *mole* recipe on page 159.

You can make the *totopos* in advance and keep them in an airtight container until needed. They should absorb the sauce, but still remain a bit crispy. The key is to serve the *chilaquiles* as soon as they are done so they keep their texture and crispiness. Adjust the spiciness if you are hungover by adding a few more chillies to the salsa – *chilaquiles* are the best hangover cure.

SERVES 4

½ red onion, thinly sliced
1 quantity Salsa *Verde* (page 88) or
   2 quantities Salsa *Roja* (page 78)
3 tablespoons grapeseed or
   vegetable oil
20 g (¾ oz/1½ tablespoons) butter
8 eggs
1 quantity *Totopos* (page 65)
120 g (4 oz) *Crema* (page 65)
10 g (¼ oz) grated Cotija or
   Pecorino cheese
freshly chopped coriander
   (cilantro) leaves, for garnish

1. First, place the thinly sliced red onion in a small bowl of cold water and set aside while you prepare the *chilaquiles*. The water will soften the raw onion taste. In Mexico, we call this process *desflemar* (page 44).

2. You will need two large frying pans (skillets). In the first, fry the salsa in the oil over a medium heat for 2–3 minutes. Meanwhile, in the second frying pan, melt the butter over a medium heat until foamy. Add the eggs and cook for about 3 minutes, or until the whites are set but the yolks are still runny.

3. When the eggs and salsa are ready, add the *totopos* to pan with the salsa and toss until well coated.

4. Quickly divide the *totopos* between the plates, then top each plate with two eggs. Garnish with dollops of *crema*, slices of red onion, and a scattering or your chosen cheese and coriander.

TIP: The recipe can easily be halved to serve two.

Hibiscus Tamales

Most traditional sweet *tamales* in Mexico City are strawberry and pineapple. I came up with these hibiscus *tamales* for my children Sebastian and Cecilia. They are are not too sweet, they contain fresh fruit, and they can be prepared in batches and frozen so they are always available for breakfast. My kids love them!

My earliest memories of sweet *tamales* are the classic strawberry *tamales* from the *puesto* (market stall) that we would buy them on the way to my primary school in Coyoacán, Mexico City.

MAKES 6

6 large dried corn husks (see Tip)
200 g (7 oz/1¾ cups) corn
   masa harina
¼ teaspoon baking powder
100 g (3½ oz) butter, melted and
   lukewarm
190 ml (61/2 fl oz/scant ¾ cup)
   Hibiscus Cordial (page 55),
   at room temperature
200 ml (7 fl oz/¾ cup) milk, at
   room temperature
100 g (3½ oz) fresh blueberries

1. Place the corn husks in a large saucepan of simmering water and leave to soften for 30 minutes.

2. Fill the bottom of a steamer with 5 cm (2 in) water and bring to the boil.

3. Meanwhile, place the *masa harina* in a large bowl. Add the baking powder and whisk until well blended.

4. Make a well in the centre of the *masa harina*. Add the melted butter and start mixing it in with your hand, gradually adding the cordial first, then the milk. Continue to mix until a dough forms with a smooth consistency and no lumps. It should be soft and slightly sticky. Work this dough well, for at least 7 minutes, until it becomes light and very malleable. You can use a stand mixer for this, or ideally a thermal mixer. Wrap in cling film (plastic wrap) or a damp tea towel and allow to rest for 10 minutes before using.

5. To make a *tamale*, place 60 g (2 oz) *masa* in the centre of one of the softened corn husks. Make a dip in the centre of the *masa* and spoon some of the blueberries into it. Fold the edges of the *masa* over the filling to form a tube. Tuck both ends of the tube in towards the centre and secure with a strand of husk or a piece of string. If the corn husk is not long enough for this, tie each end like a Christmas cracker. Repeat with the remaining ingredients to make 6 *tamales*.

6. Cook the *tamales* in the steamer for 25 minutes, then turn off the heat and leave in the steamer for another 25 minutes. Unfold and serve the *tamales* in their husks, but do not eat the husks – just use them as plates, then discard.

TIP: If your corn husks aren't big enough, you can use two overlapping husks for each *tamale*.

Huevos Divorciados

'*Divorciado*' is a term we use colloquially when referring to a dish served with the salsa on the side, or a drink with the mixer served separately. It literally translates as 'divorced'. With *huevos divorciados*, the two salsas are not even supposed to touch and are kept separated by beans. You can have one separately from the other if you cannot decide which to go for, or you can combine them according to your preference. It tastes as vibrant and satisfying as it looks.

SERVES 4

1 quantity Salsa *Roja Cruda* (page 78)
½ quantity Salsa *Verde Cruda* (page 88)
800 g (1 lb 12 oz) Avocado Black Bean *Refritos* (page 71)
8 tortillas (12 cm/4½ in in diameter; page 57)
1 tablespoon grapeseed or vegetable oil
40 g (1½ oz) butter
8 eggs
20 g (¾ oz) Cotija or Pecorino cheese, grated
½ small red onion, finely sliced
a few sprigs of coriander (cilantro)

1. Preheat the oven to 100°C/80°C fan/210°F/gas mark ¼.

2. In three separate pans, gently warm through the salsas and refried beans. Keep warm until needed.

3. Heat a large non-stick frying pan (skillet) over a low–medium heat. Lightly brush the tortillas with the oil and pan-fry each one for a minute on each side, until soft and pliable. If you like, you can fry them for a little bit longer until the edges turn crispier and firm. This gives a completely different texture – both are delicious and will work equally well for this breakfast. Wrap the warmed tortillas in a clean kitchen towel or some baking parchment and place in the oven to keep warm until needed.

4. In the same frying pan over a medium heat, melt the butter. Crack four of the eggs into the pan and cook for about 3 minutes. Transfer the eggs to an ovenproof dish and set aside in the warm oven while you fry the rest of the eggs.

5. To serve, place two tortillas on each plate, and one fried egg on each tortilla. Spoon a line of refried beans down the centre of the plate. Cover the white of one egg with warm salsa *roja* and the white of the other with warm salsa *verde*, leaving the yolks free of sauce. Garnish with grated Cotija or pecorino cheese, sliced red onion and coriander. Serve at once.

Machaca Scrambled Egg Burrita

When I first arrived in London back in 2007, burritos were a big trend. I remember having drinks at the pub with Natalie's friends from university. One of them, Hayley, told us about how she was looking forward to trying a burrito while visiting Chiapas for the first time during her gap year. She was really looking forward to the 'real deal' while in Mexico – but she couldn't find any. Back then, a lot of people were familiar with the kind of burritos we find on the UK high street, but these are Tex-Mex or Californian.

What you find in Mexico are *burritas*, which come from the north of Mexico. They are traditionally filled with a smear of beans, meat and salsa only, so they are smaller and simpler than the Tex-Mex variety, which are filled with a lot more ingredients, including rice, *pico de gallo*, soured cream, etc.

Machaca could be described as the Mexican version of beef jerky. It is traditionally found in the northern regions of Mexico: Monterrey, Sonora and Chihuahua. The beef is marinated with salt and spices and left to dry in the sun before being finely shredded. I remember my father returning from working trips to Monterrey with packs of *machaca* and wheat flour tortillas, which are more popular in the north. My mother would lightly fry the *machaca*, then add it to scrambled eggs. These were then wrapped in a wheat tortilla with a smear of refried beans – no salsa. Perfect for children, and a delicious light meal. These days, I can definitely tolerate more spiciness, so I have added a unique smoky salsa made with my favourite pasilla mixe chillies. I hope the combination makes sense to your taste buds, as this is my favourite way.

MAKES 6

250 g (9 oz) Refried Beans (page 71)

50 ml (1¾ fl oz/3 tablespoons) water

120 g (4 oz) *machaca* or beef jerky strips

2 tablespoons oil

200 g (7 oz) Onion *Sofrito*, (page 50)

3 ripe tomatoes, chopped

6 large eggs, whisked

60g (2 oz) cold butter

300 g (10 oz) Salsa Pasilla Mixe, (page 95)

6 wheat tortillas, homemade (page 62) or shop-bought

1. Place the refried beans and water in a saucepan over a medium heat and cook until heated through, stirring often and being careful not to let them burn at the bottom.

2. If you are using beef jerky strips, place them in a food processor and process until finely shredded. This might take a few minutes.

3. Heat the oil in a large frying pan (skillet) over a medium heat and fry the shredded beef pieces for a couple of minutes until slightly toasted. Add the Onion *Sofrito* and cook for 6–8 minutes until slightly caramelised. Add the chopped tomatoes and cook for 3–4 minutes until they start to disintegrate. Set aside and keep warm while you cook the eggs.

4. Pour the whisked eggs into a medium-sized saucepan and add the cold butter. Cook over a medium heat for about 5 minutes, stirring constantly with a spatula, until the eggs are scrambled and fluffy. Move the pan on and off the heat if they are cooking too fast. Add the eggs to the *machaca* mixture and remove the frying pan from the heat.

→

5. Preheat the oven to 100°C/80°C fan/210°F/gas mark ¼.

6. Heat a large, non-stick frying pan (skillet) over a low to medium heat and warm one tortilla for about 20–30 seconds on each side. Transfer the warm tortilla to a chopping board. Spoon a sixth of the refried beans in a horizontal line across the tortilla, slightly lower than the centre of the tortilla. Top the refried beans with a sixth of the *machaca* and scrambled egg mixture. Finally, drizzle a sixth of the salsa over the top (if you're making this for kids, you might prefer to leave the salsa on the side).

7. Fold both sides of the tortilla towards the centre, leaving a gap of uncovered filling in the middle. Now use your thumbs to bring up the bottom part of the tortilla to cover the filling. You will have a shape that looks like an opened envelope. Clamping your hand over the folded tortilla, pull it slightly towards you to give it a round shape. Roll it as tightly as you can into a cylinder.

8. Keep the burrita warm in the oven while you make the others. You can also slightly toast them once wrapped in a non-stick frying pan.

TIP: This recipe can easily be scaled down if you only want to make a couple of burritas.

Molletes with *Pico de Gallo*

Red Leicester cheese is coloured with annatto, the seeds of our Mexican achiote tree. When annatto seeds were imported from Central America in the 18th century, their intense colouring effect and flavour made them the ingredient of choice over the carrot or saffron that had previously been used. I like to use Red Leicester because of that historical connection.

Molletes are a very common Mexican family breakfast that kids love. They are so satisfying that I would easily have them any time of the day.

SERVES 4

1 baguette
40 g (1½ oz) butter, softened
400 g (14 oz) Avocado Black Bean *Refritos* (page 71)
400 g (14 oz) Red Leicester or Cheddar cheese, or a mixture of both, grated

FOR THE *PICO DE GALLO*

300 g (10 oz) cherry tomatoes, quartered
½ teaspoon salt
juice of 1 lime
1 small red onion, thinly sliced
2 jalapeño chillies, thinly sliced
15 g (½ oz) coriander (cilantro), chopped

1. Preheat the oven to 180°C/160°C fan/350°F/gas mark 4 and line a baking tray (pan) with baking parchment.

2. To begin making the chunky *pico de gallo*, place the quartered cherry tomatoes in a bowl and sprinkle with salt. Set aside. In a separate small bowl, pour the lime juice over the onion slices and leave to *desflemar* (page 44).

3. To prepare the *molletes*, halve the baguette lengthwise. Remove the bread inside each half to create space for the filling. Spread the hollow baguette halves with the soft butter and place on the prepared baking tray. Bake for 5 minutes until crispy.

4. Switch your oven to the grill (broil) setting on medium heat, or if you have a separate grill (broiler), preheat it to medium. Spread the black bean *refritos* inside the baguettes, then top with cheese. Grill (broil) for 5–7 minutes until the cheese is melted and slightly golden.

5. Meanwhile, finish the *pico de gallo*. Add the onion and lime juice to the bowl with the tomatoes and mix together, then stir in the jalapeños and coriander. Adjust seasoning to taste.

6. Remove the baguettes from the oven or grill. Scatter the *pico de gallo* over the top, then cut the baguettes into chunks and serve at once.

Huevos Motuleños

Originally from Yucatan, this dish shines on the menus of all good breakfast restaurants in Mexico City. Don't be scared by the amount of preparation required: remember, Mexican cooking is 'slow food' by its very nature. If you have the basic components in your refrigerator, it takes very little time to assemble. I like to serve it with smoked ham hock, but it is equally delicious with smoked bacon or cubed ham, which is how these are traditionally served in the little village of Motul in the Yucatan Peninsula.

SERVES 4

300 g (10 oz) Avocado Black Bean *Refritos* (page 71)

600 g (1 lb 5 oz) *Caldillo de Jitomate* (page 51)

25 g (1 oz) Chipotle *en Adobo* Purée (page 82)

150 g (5 oz) fresh or frozen peas

200 g (7 oz) pulled Smoked Ham Hock (page 73) or 4 smoked bacon rashers (slices)

4 corn tortillas (page 57)

1 teaspoon oil, plus extra for frying the eggs

20 g (¾ oz) butter

1 fully ripe plantain, peeled and sliced

4 eggs

150 g (5 oz) *Queso Fresco* (page 67) or feta cheese

finely chopped coriander (cilantro), to garnish

1. Heat the oven to 140°C/120°C fan/275°F/gas mark 1.

2. Reheat the black bean *refritos* and the *Caldillo de Jitomate* by warming through in separate pans. If you want a spicier *caldillo*, add the chipotle purée, to taste.

3. Cook the peas in a saucepan of boiling water for a few minutes, then drain and keep warm. Reheat the pulled ham hock in a little of its stock and keep warm, or fry the bacon and keep warm.

4. To make the *tostadas*, lightly coat the tortillas on each side with oil. Place a metal rack over a baking tray (pan) and arrange the tortillas on top. Bake for 15–20 minutes, or until crispy, turning them halfway through.

5. Meanwhile, melt the butter in a frying pan (skillet) over a low heat and fry the plantain slices for about 6 minutes or until golden outside and tender inside. Set aside and keep warm.

6. Wipe the pan, add a bit of oil and fry the eggs for a couple of minutes.

7. To serve, place a *tostada* on each serving plate, then spread some black bean *refritos* on top. Spoon some *caldillo* over the beans, making sure you are covering the edges of the tostadas, then top with an egg, some pulled ham or bacon, and peas. Crumble some fresh cheese on top and garnish with coriander. Serve straight away, before the *tostadas* lose their crispiness.

Granola with Amaranth

I love to play with texture, and this granola ticks all the boxes. I bake it at two different temperatures to get the crispiest oats, seeds and almonds, then combine them with the fluffy amaranth and moist cranberries.

MAKES 680 G (1 LB 8 OZ)

50 g (2 oz/4 tablespoons) amaranth seeds
200 g (7 oz/1½ cups) oats
100 g (3½ oz/¾ cup) pumpkin seeds
70 g (2½ oz) whole almonds
50 g (2 oz) coconut oil, melted
30 g (1 oz) dark agave syrup
100 ml (3½ fl oz/scant ½ cup) apple juice
180 g (6½ oz) cranberries

1. Preheat the oven to 140°C/120°C fan/275°F/gas mark 1. Line a baking tray (pan) with baking parchment.

1. First, make the puffed amaranth. Place a small saucepan over a medium to high heat. Once it's hot, spread half of the amaranth seeds across the base of the pan and wait for them to pop – it should happen quickly. If they don't pop, your pan is not hot enough, so wipe it and start again. Once they start popping, shake the pan to make sure all the seeds pop and nothing burns. Remove the puffed seeds from the pan and repeat with the remaining seeds. Set aside.

2. Combine the oats, pumpkin seeds, almonds, coconut oil, agave and apple juice together and mix well.

3. Transfer the mixture on to the prepared baking tray and bake for 30 minutes, stirring every 10 minutes. Then reduce the oven temperature to 100°C/80°C fan/215°F/gas mark ¼ and bake for another 40 minutes. Leave the tray in the oven, with the door slightly ajar, until the mix is completely cool, around 15 minutes.

4. Remove from the oven and stir in the amaranth and cranberries, then leave to cool. It will keep well in an airtight container for 2 weeks.

Amaranth and Coconut Porridge

Amaranth is gluten-free and high in protein, manganese and magnesium. What could be better for breakfast? It is an indigenous crop to Mexico, praised by the Aztecs and used as an offering to the gods. Amaranth is now back in trend and classified as a superfood. Serve it like porridge, with the toppings of your choice – try the Hibiscus Compote on page 55 and a sprinkle of the Granola with Amaranth (see opposite) for crunchiness.

SERVES 2

200 g (7 oz/1 cup) amaranth seeds
800 ml (28 fl oz/3¼ cups) coconut water
2 cm (½ in) piece of fresh ginger root, peeled and grated
2 star anise
½ cinnamon stick
pinch of salt

TO SERVE
Hibiscus Compote (page 55)
Granola (page 138)
your choice of dried fruits, nuts and seeds

1. Place all the porridge ingredients in a medium-sized saucepan over a high heat. Bring to the boil, then reduce the heat to low and simmer for 35–40 minutes, stirring occasionally, making sure nothing sticks to the bottom. The amaranth should be tender and the mixture should have the consistency of porridge. Add a little more coconut water if you want it thinner.

2. Remove the star anise and cinnamon and serve with your choice of topping.

LUNCH

Comida

Lunch in Mexico City is the main meal of the day and takes place around 3pm. The entire city grinds to a halt for a couple of hours, and virtually everyone leaves their places of work for a leisurely, drawn-out meal. *Fondas* across the city serve home style cooking as part of their *comida corrida*, or meal of the day. Lunch consists of a starter of soup or pasta, followed by a traditional lunchtime dish such as meatballs in chipotle sauce, and a dessert like rice pudding or flan. This is always accompanied by *aguas frescas* of tamarind, horchata or hibiscus or any other fruit that is in season. The prices are exceptionally reasonable, for many it's food they would eat at home and the daily changing menu ensures your main meal of the day is filling, varied and substantial.

I can't go to Mexico City without having lunch at least once at Contramar. The restaurant serves the freshest seafood from Mexico's coastal regions. These including the signature tuna tostadas, *pescado a la talla* and many other delights. The buzz of the vibrant dining room, the consistency of the food and the impeccable service make it a joy to visit every time. And it never disappoints.

For me one of the best places to have lunch is in one of Mexico City's markets. Filled with rows and rows of fruit and vegetables, as well as an exceptional array of pinatas for children's festivities, lunch at the market is a cultural immersion in itself. On our last visit to Coyoacán market we ended up with a life size pinata of a cartoon character that my son Sebastian insisted on taking back to the UK with us, and we only stopped off for some tostadas! My absolute favourite are pig's trotter tostadas, pickled and served with shredded lettuce, cream and cheese. And no visit to a Mexican market is complete without enjoying a Mexican prawn (shrimp) cocktail. Expertly prepared in front of you and eaten at the counter, this is a dish that is as emblematic of Mexico City as of anywhere on Mexico's coast.

Sopa de Tortilla

One of the beauties of *sopa de* tortilla is its versatility. Also called *sopa Azteca*, this is a soup that can easily be turned into a family meal. The idea is to put all the toppings on the table and let everyone make their own version. As a guideline, I have listed some of the traditional toppings below, but more fried tortillas and chillies can be added, or even some *chicharrón* – crispy deep-fried pork rind.

SERVES 4

300 ml (10 fl oz/1¼ cups) vegetable oil, for frying
200 g (7 oz) tortillas, shop-bought or homemade (page 57)
750 g (1 lb 10 oz) *Caldillo de Jitomate* (page 51)
375 ml (12½ fl oz/1½ cups) Chicken Stock (page 72)
375 g (13¼ oz) shredded cooked chicken
35 g (1¼ oz) Chipotle *en Adobo* Purée (page 82)

TO GARNISH

1 avocado, peeled, stoned and finely diced
100 g (3½ oz) soured cream
100 g (3½ oz) *Queso Fresco* (page 67) or feta
½ dried ancho chilli, very finely sliced
handful of coriander (cilantro) leaves

1. Heat the oil in a sauté pan over a medium to high heat until it reaches 170°C (340°F).

2. Cut the tortillas into strips measuring 1 cm (½ in) wide and 6 cm (2½ in) long. Fry these in the hot oil in batches, then leave to drain on paper towels. Set aside.

3. In a large saucepan over a medium heat, simmer the *caldillo*, chicken stock and shredded chicken for 10–15 minutes. Gradually add the chipotle *en adobo* purée, testing after each addition, until you are happy with the spiciness.

4. Place some fried tortilla ribbons at the bottom of a soup bowl and ladle some of the *caldillo* mixture over the top. Garnish with diced avocado, a spoonful of soured cream, some crumbled *queso fresco* or feta, a little ancho chilli, some torn coriander leaves and a few extra fried tortilla ribbons. Repeat for the other bowls and serve at once.

Watercress and Radish Salad with Puffed Amaranth

Radishes were not my favourite as a kid. I have learnt to appreciate them over the years, though, and their peppery taste mixes perfectly with a citrusy dressing. This is a particularly simple and refreshing summer salad, sprinkled with crispy puffed amaranth for even more crunchiness.

SERVES 4

1 watermelon radish, thinly sliced with a mandoline or sharp knife
10 breakfast radishes, halved or quartered
100 g (3½ oz) watercress
100 g (3½ oz) rocket (arugula)
1 avocado, peeled, stoned and sliced
150 g (5 oz) cherry tomatoes

FOR THE PUFFED AMARANTH
20 g (¾ oz/1¾ tablespoons) amaranth seeds

FOR THE DRESSING
100 ml (3½ fl oz/scant ½ cup) grapefruit juice
50 ml (1¾ fl oz/3 tablespoons) lemon juice
1½ tablespoons cider vinegar
½ teaspoon honey
¼ teaspoon salt
150 ml (5 fl oz/scant ⅔ cup) extra virgin olive oil
10 g (½ oz) mint leaves, finely chopped

1. Begin by making the puffed amaranth. Preheat a small saucepan over a medium–high heat. Once it's hot, spread half of the amaranth seeds across the base of the pan and wait for them to pop – it should happen quickly. If they don't pop, your pan is not hot enough, so wipe it and start again. Once they start popping, shake the pan to make sure all the seeds pop and nothing burns. Remove the puffed seeds from the pan and repeat with the remaining seeds. Set aside.

2. To make the dressing, combine the citrus juices, vinegar, honey and salt in a bowl or jug and whisk until well blended. Slowly add the olive oil, whisking until the mixture is emulsified. Set aside.

3. Arrange the radishes, watercress, rocket, avocado and tomatoes on 4 plates. Drizzle each with some dressing and garnish with the puffed amaranth. Serve with any remaining dressing on the side.

Heirloom Tomato Salad with Cacao and Agave Dressing

I originally created this salad dressing for fresh tomatillos, but it is also delicious with tomatoes, especially in the summer when ripe multi-coloured heirloom tomatoes appear in the markets. The dressing is a simple mixture of balsamic vinegar, agave syrup and cacao nibs. If you leave it to infuse for a few days, the cacao nibs release their complex flavour, like a vintage liqueur.

SERVES 4

½ small fennel bulb
500 g (1 lb 2 oz) heirloom tomatoes
  – choose assorted shapes
  and colours
1 teaspoon ancho chilli flakes
extra virgin olive oil, for drizzling
salt
coriander (cilantro) leaves,
  to garnish

FOR THE DRESSING

100 ml (3½ fl oz/scant ½ cup)
  balsamic vinegar
100 ml (3½ fl oz/scant ½ cup) dark
  agave syrup
6 tablespoons cacao nibs

1. Prepare the dressing at least a day in advance. Mix together the balsamic vinegar, agave syrup and cacao nibs in a jar and leave at room temperature to infuse.

2. To make the salad, remove the fennel's coarse outer leaves, then halve the bulb and remove the core. Thinly slice the fennel bulb, then leave to soak in cold water for 30 minutes. The cold water will make the fennel even more crunchy.

3. Cut the tomatoes into wedges and quarter the smaller ones. Sprinkle with salt and leave aside. The salt will draw the juices from the tomatoes, releasing their sweet flavour, while the slight acidity from the juices will complement the dressing.

4. To assemble the salad, place the tomatoes and their juices in a serving bowl. Add the sliced fennel and about 3 tablespoons of the dressing. Gently toss, then drizzle with olive oil and sprinkle with the ancho chilli flakes and coriander leaves. Serve at once.

Seafood Cocktail

This seafood cocktail is a classic in well-established *marisquerias* in Mexico City, probably because it reminds us of holidays by the coast, so enjoying it in the city is a culinary dream. Keep the sauce in the refrigerator or on ice and mix the ingredients just before serving.

SERVES 4

2 tablespoons salt
3 bay leaves
8 large king prawns (shrimp), left whole
8 sushi-grade scallops
2 avocados, peeled and stoned, 1 sliced and 1 diced
Tostadas (page 186) or crackers, to serve

FOR THE COCKTAIL SAUCE
200 g (7 oz/¾ cup) tomato ketchup
½ red onion, finely chopped
½ jalapeño chilli, finely chopped
1 teaspoon Worcestershire sauce
½ teaspoon Tabasco sauce
3½ tablespoons tomato juice
1¾ tablespoons lime juice
3½ tablespoons orange juice
3–4 sprigs of coriander (cilantro), finely chopped, plus whole leaves to garnish
pinch of salt
pinch of freshly ground black pepper

1. Begin by making the cocktail sauce. Mix together all the ingredients in a bowl and set aside in the refrigerator until you are ready to serve.

2. Bring 2 litres (70 fl oz/8 cups) of water to the boil in a large saucepan and add the salt and bay leaves. Add the prawns and simmer for 3–4 minutes, depending on their size.

3. Meanwhile, fill a large bowl with water and ice cubes. When the prawns are cooked, drain and immediately plunge them into the iced water to stop the cooking process. Drain again.

4. Peel the prawns, then slice each in half lengthways and remove any black veins. Reserve 4 halves for garnish, and roughly chop the rest. Halve the scallops horizontally, then quarter.

5. Place the chopped prawns, chopped scallops and cocktail sauce in a bowl and mix until well blended. Add the diced avocado and mix gently, being careful not to break up the avocado. Taste and adjust seasoning.

6. Divide the mixture between 4 serving glasses and garnish each one with avocado slices, coriander leaves and a prawn half. Serve with *tostadas* or crackers.

Lentil Soup with Plantain and Pancetta

This is a simple, healthy soup that your kids will love. It reminds me of home and brings back early memories of comfort food. The sweetness of the buttered fried plantain and the smokiness of the pancetta enhance the earthy flavour of the lentils. My *Abuela* Carmela's finishing touch was freshly chopped parsley and finely chopped *pico de gallo*.

SERVES 4

200 g (7 oz/1 cup) brown lentils
2 bay leaves
2 garlic cloves, peeled
1 onion, quartered
800 ml (28 fl oz/3¼ cups) water
2 tablespoons olive oil
35 g (1¼ oz) *Mojo de Ajo* (page 49)
500 ml (17 fl oz/2 cups) *Caldillo de Jitomate* (page 51)
small bunch of fresh flat-leaf parsley, chopped
¾ teaspoon salt
20 g (¾ oz) butter
1 plantain, peeled and chopped
150 g (5 oz) pancetta or smoked bacon, cubed
Pico de Gallo (page 133), optional

1. Place the lentils, bay leaves, garlic cloves and a quarter of the onion in a saucepan. Add 600 ml (20 fl oz/2½ cups) of water and 1 tablespoon of the olive oil. Bring to a boil and simmer for 15 minutes until the lentils are tender and the water has been absorbed.

2. Meanwhile, thinly slice the rest of the onion. Heat the remaining olive oil in a second saucepan over a low heat. Add the *Mojo de Ajo* and sliced onion and cook for 10 minutes, then add the *Caldillo de Jitomate* and bring to a simmer.

3. Remove the onion quarter and garlic cloves from the lentils. Stir in the *caldillo* mixture, along with half of the parsley and 200 ml (7 fl oz/scant 1 cup) of water. Simmer for 10 minutes, then add the salt. Taste and adjust seasoning if needed.

4. Just before serving, prepare the garnish. Melt the butter in a medium-sized frying pan (skillet) over a low heat, then add the plantain and fry for about 6 minutes until soft and slightly caramelised. Remove from the pan and keep warm. Keeping the pan on the heat, add the pancetta or bacon and fry for 3–4 minutes until crispy.

5. Serve the soup garnished with the plantain, pancetta and remaining parsley, and, if you like, some *pico de gallo*, just like my grandma.

Hibiscus Flower Enchiladas

Once you are used to preparing this enchilada salsa, I encourage you to try it with different kinds of chillies. I personally love the flavour of meco chipotle chillies from the state of Puebla. They have a unique smokiness and texture. My local *bodega* in New York – Mi Barrio in Bushwick – where we used to get our groceries, genuinely satisfied the demand for Puebla produce in the city. No wonder Mexicans and New Yorkers call the city Puebla York: the Puebla population there is huge, as is their culinary influence.

SERVES 2

¼ red onion, thinly sliced
6 tortillas, shop-bought or
    homemade (page 57)
oil, for brushing
1 quantity hibiscus flower filling
    (page 176)
180 g (6½ oz) *Queso Fresco*
    (page 67)
coriander (cilantro) leaves,
    to garnish

FOR THE ENCHILADA SALSA
500 g (1 lb 2 oz) tomatoes
1 large onion, quartered
3 red or green jalapeño chillies
8 garlic cloves, peeled
150 ml (5 fl oz/scant ⅔ cup) water
1 tablespoon oil
100 g (3½ oz) *Crema* (page 65)
¾ teaspoon salt

1. Place the thinly sliced red onion in a small bowl of cold water and set aside.

2. To make the salsa, place a *comal* or large, heavy-based frying pan (skillet) over a medium to high heat and add the tomatoes, onion, jalapeños and garlic. Roast for 20–30 minutes until charred and soft. Alternatively, you can roast the vegetables in an oven preheated to 200°C/180°C fan/400°F/gas mark 6 for 30–40 minutes. Leave to cool, then place the roasted vegetables in a blender. Add the water and blend until smooth.

3. Preheat the oven to 100°C/80°C fan/210°F/gas mark ¼.

4. Heat the oil in a medium-sized saucepan. Add the blended vegetables and simmer for 10–15 minutes until slightly reduced. Stir in the *crema* and salt and simmer for 5 minutes, stirring constantly. Taste and adjust the seasoning. Keep warm while you prepare the quesadillas.

5. Place a large frying pan over a low–medium heat. Lightly brush the tortillas with oil. Take the first tortilla and fry for about 30 seconds on each side until soft and pliable. Cover half of the tortilla with about 30 g (1 oz) of hibiscus flower filling, then top with about 15 g (½ oz) of *queso fresco*. Fold the tortilla and fry for 2–3 minutes on each side until the cheese has softened and the tortilla are crispy. Transfer to an ovenproof dish in the oven to keep warm while you prepare the other tortillas.

6. Place three crispy quesadillas on each plate and top with a generous ladle of creamy salsa. Drain the sliced onion and scatter it over the quesadillas, along with some coriander leaves.

7. Serve at once.

Baja-style Fish Tacos

A classic from Baja California but now widely available anywhere in Mexican territory, from Ensenada to Tulum, with restaurants around the world replicating this Baja-style fish more and more in their menus. Because corn tortillas are naturally gluten free, I wanted to create a completely gluten-free fish taco. I find that gluten-free flour and gluten-free beer, in addition to tequila or vodka, made the fried fish fillet particularly crispy and airy.

For the salad, I use chayote, known as chow chow in Asian cooking. Fresh and crunchy, it's not a recipe that you will get tired of. However, if you want to try something slightly different at any time, try substituting the chipotle mayonnaise for the Jalapeño and Lime Mayonnaise (page 186) or, even better – and my favourite – tamarind sauce (page 190).

MAKES 12

1 litre (34 fl oz/4 cups) oil, for frying
600 g (1 lb 5 oz) skinned haddock
    fillets
12 tortillas

FOR THE BATTER

150 g (5 oz/1 cup plus
    2 tablespoons) gluten-free flour,
    plus 50 g (2 oz/scant ½ cup)
    extra for coating
½ teaspoon baking powder
½ teaspoon dried oregano
½ teaspoon salt
1 teaspoon Dijon mustard
1 tablespoon vegetable oil
1 tablespoon tequila (or vodka)
about 150 ml (5 fl oz/scant ⅔ cup)
    gluten-free beer

FOR THE PICO DE GALLO

120 g (4 oz) tomatoes, deseeded
    and finely chopped
30 g (1 oz) red onion, finely
    chopped
20 g (¾ oz) green jalapeño chilli,
    finely chopped
10 g (½ oz) coriander (cilantro),
    finely chopped
7 g (¼ oz) mint, finely chopped

FOR THE CABBAGE SALAD

120 g (4 oz) red cabbage, thinly sliced
120 g (4 oz) chayote or cucumber,
    cut into thin strips
juice of 1 large lemon
salt, to taste

FOR THE CHIPOTLE MAYO

200 g (7 oz/1 cup) mayonnaise
50 g (2 oz) Chipotle en Adobo
    Purée (page 82)
juice of ½ lime

1. Begin by preparing the batter. Combine all the ingredients in a bowl and whisk until well blended. It should have the consistency of single (light) cream: add a bit more beer if needed. Set aside.

2. Prepare all the ingredients for the *pico de gallo* and combine in a serving bowl. Set aside.

3. Prepare the vegetables for the cabbage salad, but keep them in separate bowls for now – they will be mixed at the last minute. Combine the ingredients for the chipotle mayonnaise and set aside.

4. To cook the fish, heat the oil in a large saucepan until it reaches 180°C (350°F). Preheat the oven to 120°C/100°C fan/250°F/ gas mark ½.

5. Slice the haddock diagonally into long, thin fillets of about 50 g (2 oz) each. Place the extra flour on a plate and lightly dust each fillet with flour, then dip into the beer batter before frying in the hot oil for 2–3 minutes. You can fry about 4 fillets at a time. Remove from the oil and drain on paper towels. Keep warm in the oven while you fry the remaining fillets.

6. When ready to serve, reheat the tortillas in a frying pan (skillet), lightly coating them with oil. Mix the ingredients for the cabbage salad and season with the salt and lemon to taste.

7. Place the fried fish fillets, tortillas, red cabbage salad, *pico de gallo* and chipotle mayonnaise on the table and let your guests assemble their own tacos. Put some cabbage salad on a tortilla, top with a fried fish fillet and a spoonful of mayonnaise, and garnish with *pico de gallo*. Enjoy!

Tacos *Dorados* with *Mole* 'en Chinga'

'*En chinga*' is Mexican slang for 'fast' or, more accurately, 'in a f★★★ing hurry'. Not appropriate words for some, but being in a hurry is basically a way of life in Mexico City. The expression has a complicated background that I prefer to leave for a different book, as even in Mexico it is controversial. It could be a verb, noun, adverb or adjective; it could be encouraging or completely tragic. In *El Laberinto de la Soledad*, Octavio Paz described it as having a 'magic ambiguity'. When I use the phrase here, I just want to express that this is probably the quickest way in which you can replicate the traditional *mole* flavours at home and almost from scratch. *En chinga*. And a note about plantains – you need to ensure these are really ripe, and not green.

To prepare traditional *mole*, with all its versions, influences and origins, is a long labour of love: days and days of roasting, charring, frying, milling, grinding and cooking – a true example of slow food and family traditions. *Mole* means it is a special occasion. This recipe is for a quick version of *mole* that you can prepare at home over the course of a relaxed afternoon, using widely available nut butters and tahini to speed up the process, producing a wonderfully smooth *mole* with just the right balance of flavours. It is important to use a high-quality dark chocolate, an ingredient as complex as any spice. This *mole* can be prepared in advance, and makes twice the amount of sauce needed for the *tacos dorados*. You can use the other half in *chilaquiles*, *tamales*, or as a sauce for poached chicken. It will keep well for up to 1 week, and you can even freeze it.

SERVES 4

FOR THE *MOLE*

30 g (1 oz) pasilla mixe chillies,
  trimmed and deseeded
10 g (¼ oz) ancho chillies, trimmed
  and deseeded
½ cinnamon stick, broken
  into shards
2 cloves
2 star anise
2 large tomatoes
½ white onion
4 garlic cloves, peeled
2 tablespoons butter
1 very ripe plantain, peeled
  and chopped
90 g (3¼ oz) raisins
2 tablespoons black or white tahini
2 tablespoons peanut butter
2 tablespoons almond butter
45 g (1½ oz) 100 per cent
  unsweetened dark (bittersweet)
  chocolate, finely chopped
2 tablespoons grapeseed or
  vegetable oil
brown sugar, to taste
sea salt

FOR THE TACOS DORADOS

100 g (3½ oz) Onion *Sofrito*
  (page 50)
400 g (14 oz) cooked chicken
20 tortillas (12 cm/4½ in diameter),
  shop-bought or homemade
  (page 57)
6 tablespoons grapeseed or
  vegetable oil, plus extra for
  brushing the tortillas

TO GARNISH

4 generous tablespoons *Crema*
  (page 65)
2 teaspoons sesame seeds,
  toasted
1 small red onion, thinly sliced

You will need 20 cocktail sticks
  (toothpicks)

1. Begin by making the *mole*. Place a *comal* or a heavy non-stick frying pan (skillet) over a medium to high heat and toast the chillies for about 30 seconds on each side until pliable. Place them in a bowl and cover with 500 ml (17 fl oz/2 cups) of boiling water. Leave to soak for 1 hour.

2. Meanwhile, in the same pan, toast the cinnamon shards, cloves and star anise for 30 seconds, then set aside.

3. Keeping the pan on the heat, add the tomatoes, onion and garlic and roast for 30–35 minutes until charred and soft. Alternatively, you can roast them in an oven preheated to 200°C/180°C fan/400°F/gas mark 6 for 30–40 minutes. Remove from the *comal* or oven and allow to cool. I like to deglaze the *comal* with 50 ml (1¾ fl oz/3 tablespoons) of water to get a more intense, smoky flavour.

4. Melt the butter in a small frying pan over a medium heat. Add the plantain and fry for 6–7 minutes until caramelised. Transfer to a plate and set aside. Add the raisins to the pan and cook for a couple of minutes until puffed. Set aside.

5. Place the tomatoes and garlic in a blender, along with the smoky juices from the pan. Add the chillies and their soaking water, plus the cinnamon shards, cloves and star anise. Blend until smooth. Add the plantain, raisins, tahini, peanut butter, almond butter and chocolate and blend again until smooth. If your blender is not big enough, do this in batches.

6. Heat the oil in a saucepan and fry the *mole* over a low–medium heat for 15–20 minutes until it thickens but remains pourable. Check the seasoning and adjust accordingly, adding the sugar or salt if needed, balancing its sweetness, smokiness and spiciness.

7. Preheat the oven to 100°C/80°C fan/210°F/gas mark ¼. Place the thinly sliced red onion in a small bowl of cold water and set aside.

8. Heat a large frying pan over a low heat and cook the *onion sofrito* until it sizzles. Add the chicken and cook for 5–7 minutes, stirring, until well blended and warm. Set aside.

9. Clean the frying pan and return it to the heat. Lightly brush the tortillas with oil and pan-fry in batches until soft and pliable. Working quickly, fill each tortilla with about 25 g (1 oz) of chicken mixture, then roll into a taco and secure with a cocktail stick along the length of the taco – this makes it easier to fry without them falling apart.

10. When all the tortillas are filled, heat 3 tablespoons oil in a large frying pan and fry half of the soft tacos for a couple of minutes on each side until golden and crispy. Transfer them to an ovenproof dish and keep warm in the oven while you fry the other half of the tacos with the remaining 3 tablespoons oil. You now have chicken tacos *dorados*.

11. To serve, drain the red onion, then place 5 tacos *dorados* on each plate, pour some *mole* over the top, and garnish with a spoonful of *crema*, some toasted sesame seeds and some finely sliced red onion. Make sure you have plenty of napkins nearby, as these deliciously addictive tacos are messy.

Ox Tongue Tacos

This is one of my favourite tacos. It's probably the taco I crave the most while I'm not in Mexico City, and the one that I make the most at home, because Natalie also loves them. These tacos are still one of the best sellers at Santo Remedio from the specials board.

My mum prepares ox tongue sliced and grilled and then serves it with Pipián Verde (page 240), probably my dad's favourite dish – so it's genuinely long running family favourite.

Cooking ox tongue requires patience, love and practise; make sure you ask your butcher in advance, and get the best quality that you can.

FOR 20 TACOS

20 corn tortillas, shop-bought or homemade (page 56)
1 tablespoon grapeseed or vegetable oil
4 limes, cut into wedges
coriander (cilantro) leaves, chopped, to garnish
red onion, finely chopped, to garnish
Salsa *Verde Cruda* (page 88) and/or Salsa *de Árbol* (page 92), to serve

FOR THE OX TONGUE

1 whole ox tongue (around 1 kg/ 2 lbs 3 oz), washed and trimmed
300 g (10 ½ oz) rock salt
6 bay leaves
2 red onions, halved
1 tablespoon grapeseed or vegetable oil
juice of ½ lime
1 teaspoon of sea salt
freshly ground black pepper

1. Cover the ox tongue with about 3 litres (101 fl oz/12 cups) of cold water. Weigh it down with a plate, making sure the tongue is submerged. Leave to soak for 24 hours in the refrigerator, changing the water about four times over the course of this period, replacing the plate each time.

2. Combine the rock salt with a further 3 litres (101 fl oz/12 cups) in a large pan. Bring to simmer, stirring all the time until the salt is dissolved. Remove from the heat and leave to cool.

3. Drain and rinse the ox tongue. Cover with the prepared brine, making sure it is submerged and leave in the refrigerator overnight.

4. The next day, rinse the tongue and place it in a large saucepan. Cover with cold water and bring to a boil. As soon as it has reached its boiling point, reduce to a simmer, add the bay leaves and red onions and cook slowly for 3–4 hours. The tongue is cooked when a knife can easily be inserted into the flesh. Remove from the heat and leave to cool.

5. When it is cool enough to handle, peel off and remove all of the skin. Make sure you do this when the tongue is still warm and do it gently to avoid damage when pulling to quick when peeling. It is almost impossible to do it when the tongue is cold.

6. Slice the tongue and then chop into 1 cm (½ in) cubes.

7. In a saucepan over a medium high heat and fry the cubed ox tongue until beginning to crisp, around 5 minutes. Season with the lime, salt and pepper, moving constantly. Check seasoning and cook until fully crisp.

8. When ready to serve, reheat the tortillas in a frying pan, lightly coating them with oil.

9. Served the ox tongue over the warm tortillas with the limes, coriander and red onion to garnish, along with the salsa of your choice. I love to combine Salsa *Verde Cruda* and a few drops of Salsa *de* Árbol, but Natalie prefers just Salsa *Verde Cruda* on its own.

Tacos de Canasta

In Mexico City, a basket lined with a bright blue bag means tacos *de canasta* ('basket tacos'), also called tacos *sudados* ('sweaty tacos'!). These tacos are traditionally kept in a blue plastic bag in which they steam in their own heat. Adding an oily *adobo* and quickly wrapping them makes them soft, 'sweaty' and slightly oily, but delicious. One of the many stories about the origin of these traditional tacos is that they were invented in the middle of the last century in San Vicente in the state Tlaxcala: the tacos *de canasta* capital. They are cheap and extremely popular, with students, office workers and *burocratas* grabbing them at lunchtime for a quick bite on the go. One of the iconic sights of Mexico City are the *taqueros*, vendors on bicycles carrying a huge basket lined with a blue bag full of tacos, with condiments attached to the basket handle – usually an old family-size mayonnaise jar full of spicy salsa *verde* and another jar with *escabeche* or pickled onions.

Most *chilangos* would say that, without the basket and the plastic bag, it's not the real thing. I tend to agree, even though you can replicate the effect at home by steaming your tacos in plastic bags (of any colour!) to keep them warm. My little Sebastian objects to plastic bags, so at home I use large sheets of beeswax wrap, which comfortably keep half a dozen tacos sweaty.

These tacos are definitely my children's favourites, and a very easy and quick option for lunch or dinner, as you don't necessarily need to prepare all three fillings in one go. My daughter Cecilia's favourite filling is *frijoles*, while mine has always been *chicharrón prensado*. As I'm almost 5,000 miles away from Mexico City, I think this recipe is a quick and practical alternative to the traditional one.

FOR 12 TACOS

12 tortillas, shop-bought or
homemade (page 57)
1 tablespoon grapeseed or
vegetable oil
1 teaspoon Guajillo *Adobo*
(page 89)

FOR THE *PAPAS CON CHORIZO*

2 tablespoons oil
500 g (1 lb 2 oz) potatoes, peeled
and diced
150 g (5 oz) cooking chorizo, skin
removed, chopped

FOR THE *FRIJOLES*

350 g (12 oz) Avocado Black
Bean *Refritos* (page 71)
50 g (2 oz) feta cheese

FOR THE *CHICHARRÓN PRENSADO*

160 g (5¾ oz) good-quality pork
crackling
8 tablespoons Guajillo *Adobo*
(page 89)
juice of 1 lime
20 mint leaves, chopped

TO GARNISH

1 small onion, thinly sliced
1 x quantity Orange Coleslaw
Dressing (page 223)
1 jalapeño chilli, tailed, trimmed,
deseeded and cut into strips
Chiles en Escabeche (page 46)

1. Place the onion slices in the orange dressing and leave to marinate while you prepare the fillings.

2. For the *papas con chorizo*, heat the oil in a frying pan (skillet) over a medium to high heat and add the potatoes. Fry for 15 minutes until tender and golden brown, then add the chorizo and cook for a further 5 minutes. Slightly crush the mixture, letting the oil released by the chorizo seep into the potatoes. Season to taste and set aside to keep warm in the pan.

3. For the *frijoles*, simply place the beans in a saucepan over a low heat and gently warm through, adding a bit of water if they become too dry. Set aside in the pan to keep warm.

4. Meanwhile, finely crush half the crackling and roughly chop the other half. Place the crushed and chopped crackling in a medium-sized frying pan over a medium heat. Add the *adobo* and cook for 5 minutes until fragrant. Add half the lime juice and the mint. Taste for seasoning, and add more lime if needed. Set aside in the pan to keep warm.

5. When all the fillings are ready, mix the Guajillo *Adobo* with the vegetable oil and lightly brush the mixture over the tortillas. Heat the tortillas in a large non-stick frying pan over a medium heat, warming each one for 30 seconds on each side until soft and pliable.

6. Divide the fillings between the tortillas – there will be enough for 4 tortillas of each kind. Scatter the feta over the *frijoles* tortillas, then roll into tacos. As soon as the tortillas are filled and rolled, wrap them in a plastic or paper bag to keep warm and 'sweaty'. Serve with the marinated onions, fresh chilli strips and *Chiles en Escabeche* – just like in Mexico City.

Pambazo

Pambazo is one of the most delicious sandwiches. It is the ultimate street food; an explosion of taste in the mouth – and in the hands! Many serviettes are required. What makes the *pambazo* unique is the red *telera* bread, which is pan-fried in Guajillo *Adobo*. I love to serve this sandwich with leftover roasted potatoes, grilled chorizo sausages and a generous dollop of chipotle *crema*. It is a bit of a production, but you won't regret it.

MAKES 8

8 tablespoons *Crema* (page 65)
2 tablespoons Chipotle *en Adobo* Purée (page 82)
2 tablespoons butter
400 g (14 oz) leftover roasted potatoes, crushed
8 chorizo sausages, split open lengthways
200 g (7 oz) Cheddar or Monterey Jack cheese, grated
8 *Telera* breads (page 63)
100 g (3½ oz) Guajillo *Adobo* (page 89)
3 tablespoons oil
100 g (3½ oz) lettuce, chopped
120 g (4 oz) *Cebolla Morada* (page 52)

1. In a bowl, mix together the *Crema* and Chipotle *en Adobo* Purée until well blended. Set aside.

2. Melt the butter in a frying pan (skillet) over a low heat, then add the crushed roasted potatoes and warm through. Set aside and keep warm. Keeping the frying pan on the heat, add the chorizo sausages, split side-down, and cook for 5 minutes, then turn over and cook for 5 minutes on the other side.

3. Meanwhile, brush the *Telera* buns with the Guajillo *Adobo*. Heat the oil in a separate frying pan over a medium heat and fry the buns for 1 minute on each side until slightly charred and soft. Do this in batches, frying 4 at a time. Set aside, and once they've cooled just enough to handle, split them open with a bread knife.

4. Preheat the grill (broiler) to medium and line a baking tray (pan) with tin foil (aluminum foil).

5. Place 50 g (2 oz) of crushed potatoes on the bottom half of each bun, top with a chorizo sausage and sprinkle with 25 g (1 oz) cheese. Arrange all the buns on the prepared baking tray and place under the grill for 2–3 minutes until the cheese is melted.

6. Place the buns on a warmed serving platter and arrange the lettuce and *Cebolla Morada* on the top of the cheese. Spread the top half of each bun with chipotle *crema* and press lightly on top of each *pambazo*. Serve straight away while still hot.

SNACKS

Antojitos

Snacks in Mexico City are sold by street vendors, and are enjoyed by those with a lack of time between meals because of commuting, but also in social settings, such as outside churches or main parks. When I was a child, weekly church attendance with my family was an hour spent daydreaming about which snacks I would get to enjoy from the vendors waiting outside. Would it be a quesadilla with *chicharron*, an empanada chicken *tinga*, or some *sopes* with black beans and cheese topped with chorizo? With such dilemmas as these as a child there was no time for me to spend the hour contemplating anything more existential or esoteric.

My favourite place to spend an afternoon enjoying typical Mexican snacks is in squares like San Angel. Here you can enjoy a leisurely stroll on a Saturday afternoon with your snack of choice while listening to street musicians or looking at artwork on sale in the plaza, before passing some time at the Bazar del Sabado which sells Mexican crafts, silver jewellery from the mining town of Taxco and beautiful hand woven rugs. My snack of choice are *esquites*, corn kernels charcoal-grilled or boiled with epazote and árbol chilllies, and topped with mayo, lime, chilli and cheese. There is simply no snack that is more Mexican than this.

With thousands of street vendors, there is an opportunity to stop for a snack on almost every corner of Mexico City. Before the Covid-19 pandemic there were 10,000 places in Mexico selling tacos or *tortas* alone. The smell of quesadillas, tacos and other Mexican *antojitos* wafts through the streets and is impossible to resist – as are the vendors, with their stalls expertly set up to entice passers-by in a city where the competition is rife.

Bright lights, colourful hand-painted signs and the smoke and smell of sizzling meat all combine to make stopping irresistible, even if you are not hungry! The streets of this city truly are a culinary *smorgasbord*.

Mexican *antojitos* are eaten by hand – no cutlery is involved, just like in pre-Hispanic times. I genuinely feel that there is more of a connection with the earth when we eat food by hand. Just heaven.

Hibiscus Flower Quesadillas

Not all hibiscus bushes are edible. Hibiscus *sabdariffa*, also called Roselle, is the variety traditionally used in cooking. It is actually the calyxes and not the flowers which are dried and used to make hibiscus juice, cordial or tea. In my cooking, nothing is wasted, so once they have been used for infusion, I like to use the sour berry-like calyxes as a filling for quesadillas or enchiladas. This is not a traditional Mexican filling, but I think it makes a delicious, crunchy and interesting option for a simple vegetarian, zero-waste quesadilla.

You might think that all quesadillas must be filled with cheese (*queso*) – however, this is not the case in Mexico's capital. It is still a cultural and urban debate among *tragónes* and street food purists, so it's ok to be confused. When visiting a quesadilla stand in Mexico City, be prepared to be asked '*Con queso o sin queso, joven?*' ('With cheese or without cheese, young man?') after ordering from a huge variety of *guisados* (fillings) on offer, such as *chicharrón prensado*, *huitlacoche*, mushrooms, *flor de calabaza* and many more. So you can technically order one *chicharrón prensado* with cheese and another without cheese, and both are considered quesadillas. '*Joven*' is generic: everyone is a young man in Mexico City, regardless of their age, so take advantage while visiting the capital.

SERVES 4

12 corn or wheat tortillas (12 cm/ 4½ in in diameter), store-bought or homemade (pages 57 and 62)
180 g (6½ oz) Oaxaca, Monterey Jack or mozzarella cheese, grated (optional)

FOR THE HIBISCUS FLOWER FILLING

30 g (1 oz) *Mojo de Ajo* (page 49)
2 tablespoons grapeseed or vegetable oil
100 g (3½ oz) Onion *Sofrito*, (page 50)
240 g (8½ oz) cooked hibiscus flowers (page 55)
40 g (1½ oz) Chipotle *en Adobo* purée (page 82)
60 g (2 oz) *Caldillo de Jitomate* (page 51)
1 teaspoon salt
pinch of ground white pepper

1. To make the filling, heat the *mojo de ajo* and oil in a frying pan (skillet) over a medium heat for a couple of minutes until hot. Add the onion *sofrito* and flowers and fry for 5 minutes, then add the *chipotle en adobo* purée and fry for a further 2 minutes. Finally, add the *caldillo* and fry until the *caldillo* has been absorbed and reduced. Stir in the salt and white pepper and keep warm.

If you're using fresh tortillas

Prepare the fresh tortillas and cook in a *comal* or a heavy non-stick frying pan. When the tortilla is partially cooked, add the hibiscus flower filling (or the filling of your choice), then add the grated cheese (if using) and fold the tortilla. Leave it a bit longer to allow the cheese to melt, turning occasionally, until the tortilla dough is fully cooked and the edges start to crisp.

If you're using shop-bought tortillas

Heat a large non-stick frying pan over a low–medium heat. Reheat the tortillas on both sides until they are soft and malleable enough that when you fold them, they won't break. Add the filling and cheese, then fold and cook, turning occasionally, until the cheese is melted. Quesadillas can be either really soft or slightly crispy. Like *chilaquiles*, I prefer them crispy.

Esquites

This is one my favourite snacks when I'm in Mexico City and I need a quick, healthy fix. Traditionally, *elotes* and *esquites* are sold outside churches or parks where large groups congregate. My favourites, as always, are the ones that are grilled on charcoal: imagine a little *robata* grill (broiler) attached to a street cart. This recipe uses the grill in your kitchen for easy home cooking, but if you can get the barbecue going, this corn will acquire a wonderful charred flavour. Pull the husks back, remove the silky threads, then replace the husks and barbecue for 30–40 minutes, turning regularly.

SERVES 4

4 corn cobs, husks and silky
   threads removed
1 litre (34 fl oz/4 cups) water
1 onion, halved
1 árbol chilli
30 g (1 oz) fresh coriander (cilantro)
4 bay leaves
20 g (¾ oz) *Mojo de Ajo* (page 49)
1 tablespoon grapeseed or
   vegetable oil
¼ teaspoon Mexican oregano
¼ teaspoon salt

TO GARNISH

120 g (4 oz/generous ½ cup)
   mayonnaise or Chipotle Mayo
   (page 155)
20 g (¾ oz) grated Pecorino cheese
   (or Cotija, if available)
piquin powder or ground chilli
   powder

1. Preheat the grill (broiler) to maximum and line an roasting tray (pan) with tin (aluminum) foil.

2. Trim the base of each corn cob and place on the prepared tray. Grill for 20–30 minutes, turning often, until well charred on all sides. Set aside until cool enough to handle.

3. To detach the corn kernels, stand each corn cob on its trimmed base and run a knife down the cob, as close to the core as possible. Set aside.

4. Place the corn cob cores in a medium-sized saucepan, cover with the water and bring to a boil over a high heat. Add the onion, chilli, coriander and bay leaves. Reduce the heat to low and simmer, uncovered, for about 45 minutes, or until reduced by two thirds.

5. When the stock is ready, heat the *Mojo de Ajo* and oil in a medium-sized frying pan (skillet) over a medium heat until sizzling. Add the corn kernels and stir-fry for 5 minutes. Add 150 ml (5 fl oz/scant ⅔ cup) of the stock, along with the oregano and salt. Stir-fry for another 5 minutes, or until most of the stock has been absorbed and the corn is glossy.

6. Divide the mixture between four bowls, then top each bowl with mayonnaise, cheese and a pinch of piquin or chilli powder.

Queso Fundido with Rajas and Chorizo

It took me a long time to come up with the perfect combination of cheeses for this *queso fundido*. I wanted to use some of the wonderful cheese produced in the British Isles while still keeping the stringy, creamy texture of the classic Mexican *queso fundido*. I am happy with the result, and the introduction of Coolea cheese, an Irish Gouda-style cheese produced in the county of Cork, with a sweet, almost caramel-like flavour. Make sure you have plenty of *totopos* and enjoy the *queso fundido* at its best: hot and bubbly, just out of the oven.

SERVES 4–6

190 g (6¾ oz) Cheddar cheese, grated
190 g (6¾ oz) Coolea cheese, grated
250 g (9 oz) Monterey Jack cheese, grated
1 tablespoon oil
1 poblano chilli or 60 g (2 oz) padrón peppers, trimmed, deseeded and cut into thin strips
1 chorizo, casing removed, crumbled
Totopos (page 65), to serve

1. Preheat the oven to 190°C/170°C fan/375°F/gas mark 5.

2. Place all the cheeses in a bowl and mix together gently without compressing until combined. Place in a shallow ovenproof dish and bake for about 20 minutes until all the cheeses have melted and the top is turning golden.

3. Meanwhile, heat the oil in a small frying pan (skillet) over a medium to high heat. Add the strips of poblano chilli or Padrón pepper and fry for about 5 minutes until soft. Set aside and cover to keep warm. In the same frying pan, fry the chorizo crumbs for 5 minutes until crispy. Set aside and keep warm.

4. When the cheese is ready, remove it from the oven and arrange the chorizo crumbs and poblano strips on top. Serve straight away, with plenty of *totopos*.

Padrón Rajas con Crema

This is one of the most iconic vegetable *guisados* in Mexican cooking, and a must in any legitimate *taquiza*. It's traditionally prepared with poblano chillies, but these can be really hard to get hold of in the UK, so I looked for an alternative and found that Padrón peppers worked best. It is a creamy unctuous filling for tacos and pasties (page 192).

SERVES 4

1 large sweetcorn cob, or
   2 small ones
1 tablespoon vegetable oil
30 g (1 oz) *Mojo de Ajo* (page 49)
100 g (3½ oz) Onion *Sofrito*
   (page 50)
⅛ teaspoon Mexican oregano
1 teaspoon salt
⅛ teaspoon freshly ground
   black pepper
260 g (9¼ oz) Padrón peppers,
   halved and stalks removed
   (see Tip)
200 g (7 oz) *Crema* (page 65)
tortillas, to serve

1. To easily remove the husk from the corn cob(s), slice off the stem end, then pull off the husks. To detach the kernels, stand the corn cob on its cut side and run a knife down along the cob, as close as possible to the core. You will need 220 g (7¾ oz) kernels.

2. Heat the oil in a sauté pan over a medium heat. Add the *mojo de ajo* and fry until hot, making sure it does not burn. Add the *sofrito* and cook for a further couple of minutes. Now add the corn kernels, oregano, salt and black pepper and cook for about 5 minutes until the corn kernels are tender. Add the Padrón peppers and cook for a further 5 minutes until they are soft, but not so long that they completely collapse.

3. In a separate non-stick frying pan (skillet), reheat the tortillas.

4. Add the *crema* to the corn and pepper mixture and cook for 1 minute, just enough to warm it up, stirring to coat the vegetables. Taste and adjust the seasoning, then serve with the warm tortillas.

TIP: Padrón peppers are quite mild – except for the odd one – so keep the seeds.

Shiitake Mushroom Sopes

Sopes are one of the most classic dishes of the *antojitos Mexicanos* repertoire. They are made out of corn *masa* and pinched at the edges to create a raised border to contain the filling. My favourite place for sopes in Mexico City is Sopes de la Nueve, with a countless number of options to top your *sopes* – octopus, short rib, spicy cecina, the list goes on. They are filling, tasty and cheap. It started as a small shop front and became so successful that they went from serving to just a handful of customers at a time to many hundreds.

MAKES 12

½ quantity corn *masa* (page 56)
15 g (½ oz) grated Cotija or
   Pecorino cheese, to garnish

FOR THE TOPPINGS
250 g (9 oz) Avocado Black Bean
   Refritos (page 71)
3 garlic cloves, finely chopped
1 tablespoon grapeseed or
   vegetable oil
100 g (3½ oz) Onion *Sofrito*
   (page 50)
300 g (10 oz) shiitake mushrooms
6 tablespoons Guajillo *Adobo*
   (page 89)
¾ teaspoon salt
10 g (¼ oz) fresh flat-leaf parsley

1. Prepare the corn *masa* recipe and leave to rest for 30 minutes. Form the mixture into 20-g (¾-oz) balls and roll them in your hand until smooth. Using a tortilla press, flatten each one into an 8-cm (3¼-in) disc about 0.5 cm (¼ in) thick. Heat a *comal* or heavy non-stick frying pan (skillet) over a medium heat, and cook the *sopes* for about a minute on each side. They should be slightly undercooked. Remove from the pan and, while they are still warm but cool enough to handle, pinch the sides between your thumb and index finger to form little pies with raised edges.

2. When the *sopes* are ready, prepare the topping.

3. Place the black bean *refritos* in a small saucepan over a low heat and reheat for 10 minutes. Add a little water if the mixture becomes too dry.

4. Meanwhile, in a medium-sized frying pan over a medium heat, fry the garlic in the oil for 1 minute, making sure it doesn't burn. Add the onion *sofrito* and cook for a further 5 minutes until slightly coloured. Add the shiitake mushrooms and cook for 3 minutes until softened. Now add the *adobo* and cook for a couple more minutes, stirring constantly and making sure the mushrooms are well coated. Finish with the salt and parsley and keep warm.

5. Reheat the *sopes* in the *comal* or frying pan over a medium heat for 30 seconds on each side. Place on a serving platter, then divide the beans between the *sopes*. Top with the mushroom mix and garnish with Cotija or Pecorino. Serve warm.

Crab Tostadas

In Coyoacán in Mexico City, my local market has become famous for (among other things) a *tostadas* stand which has expanded and become hugely popular. The stand offers a wide variety of tostadas: chicken *tinga*, prawn (shrimp) cocktail, or *pata* (cow's hooves), which is one of my favourites.

In the UK, Cornwall is well known for the exceptional quality of its seafood, especially crab. The region is one of our favourite summer holiday destinations thanks to its beautiful landscape and beaches, as well as its culinary specialities. To pay tribute to this beautiful seafood, I like to pair it with the simple, raw freshness of a jalapeño and lime mayonnaise and serve with crispy tostadas and avocados. You don't need anything else: just delicious produce on a *tostada*. From Coyoacán to Cornwall.

SERVES 4

8 corn tortillas (12 cm/4½ in in diameter), shop-bought or homemade (page 57)
2 teaspoons grapeseed or vegetable oil
250 g (9 oz) crab meat, mixed white and brown
1 large avocado, peeled, stoned and thinly sliced
salt flakes
coriander (cilantro) leaves and lime wedges, to garnish

FOR THE JALAPEÑO AND LIME MAYONNAISE

2 jalapeños, trimmed and finely chopped
1 garlic clove, chopped
10 g (¼ oz) fresh coriander (cilantro)
14 mint leaves
100 g (3½ oz/scant ½ cup) mayonnaise
2 teaspoons lime juice

1. Preheat the oven to 170°C/150°C fan/340°F/gas mark 3½ and set a wire rack over a baking tray (pan) lined with baking parchment.

2. To make the mayonnaise, place the chopped chillies, garlic, coriander and mint in a *molcajete* (page 78) or small blender. Add a pinch of salt and crush or blend until reduced to a purée. Incorporate the chilli and herb purée into the mayonnaise, then stir in in the lime juice and taste for seasoning. Set aside.

3. To make the tostadas, lightly coat both sides of the tortillas with the oil. Arrange the tortillas on the prepared wire rack and bake for 20–30 minutes, or until crispy, turning halfway through. Sprinkle with salt flakes.

4. Place the tostadas, crab, avocado, jalapeño mayonnaise, coriander leaves and lime wedges on a serving platter and let your guests build their own tostadas: first a spread of mayonnaise, then a few avocado slices, followed by some crab meat, coriander leaves and a squeeze of lime.

Scallops *Aguachile Verde Tostadas*

In the West Pacific state of Sinaloa, scallops and prawns (shrimp) are so fresh and so sweet that they are often enjoyed raw, drizzled with a sharp chilli-infused citrus marinade called *aguachile*. You can lay the drizzled scallops on a platter, surrounded by garnishes and *tostadas* and let your guests build their own.

MAKES 6

6 corn tortillas (page 57)
1–2 teaspoons oil
6–8 sushi-grade king scallops
6 tablespoons mayonnaise
1 avocado, peeled, stoned and finely sliced
Cebolla Morada (page 52)
coriander (cilantro) leaves, to garnish

FOR THE *AGUACHILE* MARINADE

80 g (3 oz) serrano or jalapeño chillies
20 g (¾ oz) cucumber, roughly chopped
10 g (½ oz) ginger, peeled and finely chopped
1 garlic clove, peeled
50 ml (2 fl oz/3½ tablespoons) orange juice
50 ml (2 fl oz/3½ tablespoons) lemon juice
1 teaspoon sugar
1 teaspoon salt
1 teaspoon rice wine vinegar
1 teaspoon fish sauce

1. Begin by making the marinade. Place all the marinade ingredients in a blender and mix at high speed until completely smooth. Strain through a sieve (fine mesh strainer). Taste to check the seasoning and adjust accordingly. Set aside.

2. Preheat the oven to 170°C/150°C fan/340°F/gas mark 3½.

3. To make the *tostadas*, lightly coat both side of the tortillas with oil. Place on a metal rack over a baking tray (pan) and arrange the tortillas on top. Bake for 20–30 minutes, or until crispy, turning them halfway through.

4. Meanwhile, slice the scallops into very thin coins.

5. When everything is ready, place the tostadas on serving plates and thinly spread 1 tablespoon of mayonnaise over each one. Dip the scallop coins in the marinade and arrange on top of the mayonnaise, fanning them out. Garnish with the pickled onions and coriander leaves. Drizzle some of the remaining marinade over the top and serve immediately.

Tamarind Chicken Wings

Everyone loves chicken wings, and they make the perfect snack. In this recipe, the baking powder absorbs the chicken fat as they cook, making the wings extra crispy without the need for deep-frying. The tamarind marinade gives the wings a real sweet-and-sour tang with a hint of citrus, perfect to accompany the IPA of your choice for a pleasant contrast of flavours.

SERVES 4–6

2 tablespoons baking powder
1½ teaspoons salt flakes
¾ teaspoon Mexican oregano
1½ teaspoons crushed fennel seeds
1.5 kg (3 lb 5 oz) chicken wings

FOR THE TAMARIND *ADOBO*
200 g (7 oz) tamarind pulp,
   with seeds
200 ml (7 fl oz/scant 1 cup) orange
   juice
50 ml (2 fl oz/3½ tablespoons)
   lime juice
50 g (2 oz/3 tablespoons) honey
2 tablespoons soft light
   brown sugar

TO SERVE (OPTIONAL)
popcorn
tajin powder
Ancho Dry Rub (page 85)

1. Preheat the oven to 150°C/130°C fan/300°F/gas mark 2. Line a roasting tray (pan) with baking parchment.

2. To prepare the tamarind *adobo*, place the tamarind pulp and orange juice in a bowl and mix together: it is easiest to do this with your fingers. To remove the seeds, press the mixture through a sieve (fine mesh strainer). Add the lime juice directly to the sieve and continue to press and scrape. Discard the seeds and mix the honey and brown sugar into the tamarind *adobo*. Set aside.

3. In a large bowl, mix together the baking powder, salt, oregano and fennel seeds. Add the chicken wings and toss until they are well coated.

4. Spread out the wings on the prepared roasting tray and place in the oven for 30 minutes, then increase the oven temperature to 210°C/190°C fan/410°F/gas mark 6½ and bake for another 30 minutes, turning the wings half way through.

5. Reduce the oven temperature to 190°C/170°C fan/375°F/gas mark 5. Remove the tray from the oven and generously brush the wings on all sides with the tamarind *adobo*. Return to the oven for 5 minutes, then serve the wings hot. I like to serve them over a bowl of popcorn. Add an extra layer of flavour with a sprinkle of tajin powder or ancho rub, if you like. Great for a lazy Sunday afternoon snack.

Chicken *Tinga* Pasties

Tinga is a famous preparation of pulled or shredded meat in a lightly smoked tomato sauce. While usually associated with chicken, the *tinga* sauce can also be mixed with beef, or with vegetables for a vegetarian alternative (try shiitake mushrooms or even grated carrot). You can enjoy this *tinga* as a topping for tacos, *sopes* or *tostadas*, but I particularly like it as a filling for pasties.

Pasties are both British and Mexican. We pronounce them *pastes* – and obviously adapted the fillings. Cornish miners went to Mexico in the early 19th century to work in the mines: specifically to Real del Monte, a beautiful small town in the state of Hidalgo, which surrounds Mexico City. It was thanks to these Cornish miners that football was introduced to Mexico, and the country's first football club – Pachuca Athletic Club – was founded. In 2007, the Mexican Embassy in the UK named the silver mining settlements of Pachuca and Real del Monte 'Little Cornwall', and the Cornish towns of Camborne and Redruth were officially twinned with Pachuca and Real del Monte respectively.

MAKES 9

FOR THE PASTRY

375 g (13¼ oz/scant 3 cups) plain (all-purpose) flour
¾ teaspoon salt
120 g (4 oz) butter, at room temperature
1 small egg, plus 1 egg for brushing
150 ml (5 fl oz/scant ⅔ cup) IPA beer, at room temperature

FOR THE STOCK

500 g (1 lb 2 oz) chicken thighs
1.2 litres (40 fl oz/4¾ cups) water
½ small onion
1 carrot
2 cm (¾ in) piece of fresh ginger root
1 garlic clove
a few sprigs of coriander (cilantro)
1 bay leaf

1. Begin by making the pastry. Place the flour and ½ teaspoon of salt in a large bowl and whisk briefly to combine. Add the butter and rub it into the flour with your fingers. Add the egg and the IPA, a little at a time, working the mixture between each addition until the pastry comes together. The dough should be flexible and malleable. Wrap it in cling film (plastic wrap) and place in the refrigerator for 1 hour. If you wish, you can prepare it in advance and leave it in the refrigerator overnight, or even freeze it until needed.

2. Place all the stock ingredients in a large saucepan over a low heat. Bring to a simmer and cook for 40 minutes, then remove the chicken thighs from the stock and leave to cool, covered.

3. To make the *tinga* sauce, place the tomatoes and garlic in a *comal* or a heavy non-stick frying pan (skillet) over a medium to high heat and roast for 25–30 minutes until charred and soft. Alternatively, you can roast the vegetables in an oven preheated to 200°C/180°C fan/400°F/gas mark 6 for 30–40 minutes. They will not char as much, but they should still be roasted and soft. Remove from the *comal* or oven and allow to cool.

4. Place the roasted tomatoes, roasted garlic and raw onion in a blender with 300 ml (10 fl oz/1¼ cups) of the chicken stock. Blend until smooth.

FOR THE *TINGA* SAUCE

400 g (14 oz) tomatoes

2 garlic cloves, peeled

1 onion, peeled

1 tablespoon grapeseed or
vegetable oil

25 g (1 oz) Chipotle *en Adobo*
Purée (page 82)

1 large bay leaf

1 star anise

½ teaspoon Mexican oregano

½ teaspoon avocado leaf powder

¾ teaspoon salt

5. Heat the oil in a medium-sized saucepan over a medium heat. Add the blended sauce and cook for 7–8 minutes to concentrate the flavours. Add the chipotle *en adobo* purée, bay leaf, star anise, oregano and avocado leaf powder. Reduce the heat to low and simmer for 15–20 minutes until reduced and thickened. You should have about 500 ml (17 fl oz/2 cups) of sauce. Add the salt, taste and adjust seasoning. Pass the sauce through a sieve (fine mesh strainer) and leave to cool.

6. Meanwhile, remove the skin from the chicken thighs and discard, then pull the meat off the bones. Place the pulled chicken meat in a bowl and stir in half the *tinga* sauce (see Tip). Taste and adjust the seasoning, then set aside.

7. Preheat the oven to 180°C/160°C fan/350°F/gas mark 4 and line two baking trays (pans) with parchment paper. Lightly whisk the remaining egg with ¼ teaspoon salt.

8. Divide the dough into 9 portions of 50 g (2 oz) each. Roll each portion into a slightly elongated disc measuring 12 x 15 cm (4½ x 6 in) and about 0.5cm (¼ in) thick. Place about 50 g (2 oz) of chicken *tinga* filling in the centre. Brush a bit of egg around the edge and fold the pastry over. Lightly press with your fingers to seal the edges and crimp with a fork to finish. Repeat for the other pasties.

9. Arrange the pasties on the prepared baking trays and brush the top of each pasty with the egg wash mixture. Bake for 20–25 minutes until golden brown, switching the trays around halfway through baking. Serve warm.

TIP: You will only need half of the sauce, but you can freeze the other half for a second batch.

SUNDOWN DRINKS

Bebidas

arly evening in Mexico City is a magical time of the day. The sunset permeates most of the city, turning the sky a brilliant red, which is then reflected on the surrounding mountains, making for a truly breath-taking sight.

This is the time groups of friends head out for beers, cocktails or start the evening with a glass of wine. With regions like Baja California having similar *terroir* and climate to California, they produce some exceptional wines. Many are still only found in Mexico and are not available for export so when in Mexico I love to try wines we still can't source in London.

While their numbers have dwindled, *cantinas* are still very much part of the city's social fabric. When I was young I used to hear from my father how he would meet friends in a cantina for drinks, where snacks like a small *caldo de camarón* or *chistorra* sausage were bought to you with each drink you ordered. This was a space where men went to talk and drink, not the realm of children, and until 1982 even women were prohibited from entering.

I often imagined what they were like and couldn't wait for the chance to go. As is often the case once you grow up the allure was not so great once going was an option, and instead friends and I would go for drinks at local bars. But going to a *cantina* in Mexico for many is akin to going to a pub for the English or a café for the French.

On a recent trip to Mexico City we visited La Opera, where the legendary Mexican revolutionary Pancho Villa was said to have fired his gun in to the ceiling in 1910. My wife Natalie and I sat at the bar drinking tequila and mezcal respectively, while our baby daughter Cecilia slept. A fellow guest asked to take a photo, commenting on how society had evolved when as recently as the 1980s that wouldn't have been possible.

Drinks at *cantinas* are simple, but the accompanying food and the fact that they are part of the fabric of the city means I visit one every time I am in Mexico. In the early 20th century there were over a thousand in the capital and while their numbers have diminished significantly for many they are still a place to while away the hours.

For me early evening is when I like to make cocktails, to welcome friends who come to visit, before having dinner. Hand someone a hibiscus margarita or a mezcal sour and chances are if they came through the door after a tough day, within a few sips they will be feeling a lot better.

Seafood Michelada

SERVES 2

1 teaspoon oil
1 teaspoon Guajillo *Adobo* (page 89)
6 cooked king prawns (shrimp)
ice
200 ml (7 fl oz/scant 1 cup) Sangrita
  (see below), chilled
200 ml (7 fl oz/scant 1 cup) Mexican amber beer,
  chilled
celery leaves, to garnish

1. Heat the oil in a small frying pan (skillet) over
   a low heat. Add the *adobo*, followed by the
   prawns. Cook for 30 seconds on each side –
   the prawns should be well coated with *adobo*.
   Remove from the heat and thread the prawns
   on to 2 cocktail sticks (toothpicks),
   3 prawns per stick.

2. Half-fill 2 glasses with ice. Divide the sangrita
   between them, then top up each glass with
   100 ml (3½ fl oz/scant ½ cup) beer. Serve,
   garnished with celery leaves and a skewer of
   guajillo-spiced prawns.

Hibiscus Margarita

SERVES 1

ice
40 ml (1¼ fl oz) Ocho *blanco* tequila
30 ml (1 fl oz) Cointreau
25 ml (¾ fl oz) Hibiscus Cordial (page 55)
25 ml (¾ fl oz) freshly squeezed lime juice
slice of lime, to garnish

FOR THE SUGARED RIM

1 tablespoon Hibiscus Cordial (page 55)
2 teaspoons caster (superfine) sugar

1. To create a sugared rim for the cocktail glass,
   pour the hibiscus syrup on to a small plate and
   the caster sugar on to a second small plate. Dip
   the rim of a margarita glass into the syrup and
   then into the sugar, rolling the glass around to
   evenly coat the rim. Set aside.

2. Fill a cocktail shaker with ice and add the
   tequila, Cointreau, hibiscus syrup and lime
   juice. Shake well and strain into the prepared
   glass. Serve garnished with a slice of lime.

Sangrita

MAKES 1.2 LITRES (40 FL OZ/4¾ CUPS)

1 litre (34 fl oz/4 cups) tomato juice
1 teaspoon salt
1 teaspoon freshly ground black pepper
125 ml (4¼ fl oz/½ cup) orange juice
50 ml (1¾ fl oz/3 tablespoons) Valentina Mexican
  chilli sauce
25 ml (¾ fl oz/5 teaspoons) Tabasco

1. Place all the ingredients in a blender and blend
   to combine. Transfer to a jug (pitcher) and keep
   in the refrigerator until ready to use. It will
   keep for 5 days.

Cubana

SERVES 1

ice
50 ml (1¾ fl oz/3 tablespoons) Sangrita (page 201)
25 ml (¾ fl oz) lime juice
125 ml (4¼ fl oz/½ cup) Mexican amber beer, chilled

1. Half-fill a glass with ice. Add the sangrita and lime juice, then top up with beer and serve.

Mezcal Sour

SERVES 1

ice
35 ml (1¼ fl oz) Vetusto Mezcal Espadin
15 ml (1 tablespoon) amaretto
10 ml (2 teaspoons) sugar syrup
10 ml (2 teaspoons) lemon or lime juice
20 ml (1½ tablespoons) aquafaba (the liquid from a tin of chickpeas/garbanzos)
jalapeño chilli slices, to garnish

1. Fill your cocktail shaker with ice. Add the mezcal, amaretto, sugar syrup, lime juice and aquafaba and shake well. Strain into a lowball glass filled with ice and serve, garnished with 2 jalapeño slices.

Paloma

SERVES 1

ice
30 ml (1 fl oz) Don Julio Blanco tequila
25 ml (¾ fl oz) Campari
20 ml (1½ tablespoons) lime juice
125 ml (4¼ fl oz/½ cup) grapefruit tonic water
grapefruit wedge, to garnish

1. Fill a highball glass with ice, then add the tequila, Campari and lime juice. Top up with grapefruit tonic water and serve, garnished with a grapefruit wedge.

Bee's Knees

SERVES 1

ice
35 ml (1¼ fl oz) Cazcabel honey tequila
50 ml (1¾ fl oz/3 tablespoons) *Tepache* (page 112)
15 ml (1 tablespoon) freshly squeezed lime juice
orange slice, to garnish

1. Fill a lowball glass with ice, then add the tequila, Tepache and lime juice. Stir and serve, garnished with an orange slice.

DINNER

Cena

With lunch the main meal of the day, dinner for many can be a few tacos late at night after a long working day or a time to gather at home with family for dinner parties for special celebrations. Whether the speciality is carnitas, *al carbón* or *al pastor*, every family in Mexico City has their favourite *taqueria* for dinner, and they will often become life-long patron of it for generations.

I remember countless visits for tacos *al pastor* to El Tizoncito in Condesa neighbourhood. It was a treat, but also a show that I found myself mesmerised by. I would watch the *taquero* carving off thin slices of meat from the *trompo*, topped off by a piece of grilled pineapple, which he would expertly slice, and it which would fly from the top of the *trompo* and land gracefully on the taco, ready to be topped with chopped coriander and onion. The grand finale was the scoop of amazing salsa, to create the perfect taco. The beautiful dance of the taco making process was repeated time and time again, with graceful movements that spoke of repetition and respect for the trade. To ensure your tacos did not get cold you would order tacos as you went, each coming with a little square of paper, which you would pile up on your plate as you ate. At the end of the meal you would walk to the cashier and hand them your plate and were charged based on how many squares of paper you had racked up. The simplicity and trust of the system never failed.

It was probably here where I started to understand the importance of hospitality – the ambiance, the food, the ritual – and I loved it. The *taquero* welcoming you, the *taquero* serving you and the *taquero* inviting you to come back soon when leaving. All of this added to the joy of the experience. Equally I remember many a time as a child falling asleep to the sound of dinner parties at my grandparents home, complete with live music and countless relatives. Dancing, singing and a lot of food was always present and festivities went late in to the night. The supply of food was never ending and there was always plenty left over for the next days tacos when the left overs tasted even better than the night before.

When out for dinner in Mexico City I absolutely love going to the beautiful restaurant of Elena Reygadas, Rosetta. The restaurant is situated in an old house in the historic Roma neighbourhood, where the leafy streets could be mistaken for Barcelona. Elena serves her expertly prepared dishes, mixing Italian techniques with the best of Mexican ingredients. Evenings out in Mexico City don't get much better than sitting on the restaurant's patio, enjoying Mexican wine and wonderful food.

Prawns *al* Guajillo

The sauce is a very simple mix of Guajillo *Adobo* and butter with a touch of garlic. For this dish, make sure you source the best and juiciest prawns. The sauce will enhance their natural sweetness. Grilling the lime halves will add another layer of flavour, but it isn't essential.

SERVES 4

4 tablespoons oil
160 g (5¾ oz) butter
8 garlic cloves, chopped
200 g (7 oz) *Guajillo Adobo*
    (page 89)
12 best-quality large king prawns
    (shrimp), whole

TO SERVE

lemon halves, grilled (broiled)
    if possible
freshly chopped flat-leaf parsley

1. Heat 2 large frying pans (skillets) over a low to medium heat. Add 2 tablespoons oil and a quarter of the butter to each pan. When the butter is melted and foamy, divide the garlic between the 2 pans and cook for 30 seconds until just golden, being careful not to let it burn.

2. Add half the Guajillo *Adobo* to each pan and cook for a couple of minutes until hot. Then add 6 prawns to each pan and cook for 5–8 minutes depending on the size, turning them halfway through. Add the final two quarters of the butter to each pan and let it melt, stirring the sauce and prawns constantly.

3. Alternatively, if you can only use one frying pan, cook in batches, keeping the first batch warm while you cook the second.

4. Arrange the prawns on a platter and serve, garnished with grilled lemon halves and parsley.

Salmon en Mole de Frutas

This is my interpretation of a fruity *mole* that I tried once in a *fonda*. I have never had it since, I never asked for the recipe, and I didn't manage to speak to the *mayora*, but I have never forgotten it and decided to recreate it from memory here. This *mole* is rich in nuts and buttered caramelised fruits. Although I ate it served with pork ribs, I have found it is the ideal accompaniment for fish, as it gently enhances it without overpowering. It is equally delicious with pork or prawns (shrimp). I like to blend half the fruits into the *mole* and use the other half as a garnish to bring texture and tang. You will only need half of the *mole* for this dish (see Tip), but the other half can be frozen. Curing the salmon 30 minutes before grilling (broiling) will greatly improve its flavour and texture.

SERVES 4

4 salmon fillets, about 200 g (7 oz) each
2 tablespoons salt flakes
1 teaspoon sugar
1 large garlic clove, grated
about 3 tablespoons grapeseed or vegetable oil
cooked quinoa, to serve

FOR THE FRUIT MOLE

1½ guajillo chillies, trimmed and deseeded
1½ ancho chillies, trimmed and deseeded
75 g (2½ oz) almonds
2 tablespoons sesame seeds
25 g (1 oz) peanuts
3 tomatoes
1 onion, quartered
4 garlic cloves, peeled
2 tablespoons butter
½ fully ripe plantain, sliced
1 small apple, peeled and diced
1 large pear, peeled and diced
¼ pineapple, peeled and diced
150 g (5 oz) raisins
3 bay leaves
½ teaspoon ground cinnamon

1. To make the *mole*, toast the chillies in a *comal* or a heavy non-stick frying pan (skillet) over a medium to high heat until they are soft and pliable. Place the cooked chillies in a bowl and cover with 250 ml (8½ fl oz/1 cup) of boiling water. Leave to soak for 1 hour.

2. Toast the almonds in the *comal* or frying pan until golden brown. Set aside to cool, then toast the sesame seeds, followed by the peanuts. Roughly chop the almonds and peanuts.

3. Place the tomatoes, onion and garlic in the *comal* over a medium to high heat and roast for 25–30 minutes until charred and soft. Alternatively, you can roast the vegetables in an oven preheated to 200°C/180°C fan/400°F/gas mark 6 for 30–40 minutes. Remove from the *comal* or oven and allow to cool. I like to deglaze the *comal* with 50 ml (1¾ fl oz/3 tablespoons) of water for maximum smoky flavour.

4. Melt the butter in a frying pan over a medium heat, then fry the plantain for 6–7 minutes until caramelised. Remove from the heat and set aside. In the same frying pan, fry the apple, pear and pineapple for 5–6 minutes until caramelised and soft. Set aside. Finally, pan-fry the raisins for a couple of minutes, until puffed. Set aside.

5. At this stage, you can remove the salmon fillets from the refrigerator. Mix together the salt flakes, sugar and garlic and massage this mixture all over the fillets, including the skin. Cover with cling film (plastic wrap) and set aside at room temperature while you finish preparing the *mole*.

6. Place the roasted tomatoes, onion and garlic in a blender, along with the smoky *comal* juices. Add the chillies and their soaking water, and blend until smooth. Add half the nuts, plantain, apple, pear, pineapple and raisins, plus 150 ml (5 fl oz/scant ⅔ cup) of water and blend again. If your blender is not big enough, do it in batches.

7. Heat 2 tablespoons of the oil in a large saucepan over a low heat and fry the bay leaves and cinnamon for 1 minute. Add the *mole* and cook over a low–medium heat for 10–15 minutes until it thickens but remains pourable. Keep warm.

8. Preheat the grill (broiler) to medium high. Line a roasting tray (pan) with tin (aluminum) foil and lightly brush with the remaining oil. Arrange the salmon pieces on the tray, skin-side up, and grill for 10–15 minutes, depending on the thickness. They should be just cooked, with a slight translucence in the centre.

9. Arrange the salmon fillets on serving plates with the quinoa and spoon a generous ladle of *mole* over each one. Garnish with the remaining nuts and fruits. Serve with some quinoa on the side.

TIP: You will have enough *mole* for a second batch, but you will need to toast and fry more nuts and fruits for the garnish.

Mackerel
a la Talla

Pescado a la talla is a speciality from the Pacific coast. It is a butterflied fish, spread with a chilli marinade, then grilled. Although red snapper is usually the fish of choice, any fish that is suitable for grilling can be used. The iconic restaurant Contramar in Mexico City has made *pescado a la talla* their signature dish, using two different *adobos*: a red chilli base and a green herby one. This is my take on the recipe, using mackerel from the British coast.

SERVES 4

4 large mackerel, gutted and
    butterflied (ask your fishmonger
    to prepare them)
1 tablespoon grapeseed or
    vegetable oil

FOR THE GREEN MARINADE
75 g (2½ oz) flat-leaf parsley,
    roughly chopped
25 g (1 oz) Thai basil, roughly
    chopped
45 g (1½ oz) garlic, peeled and
    roughly chopped
4 tablespoons olive oil
3 tablespoons hemp oil
¼ teaspoon salt
⅛ teaspoon Mexican oregano
⅛ teaspoon ground white pepper

FOR THE RED MARINADE
120 g (4 oz) Guajillo *Adobo*
    (page 89)

TO SERVE
2 limes
Cebolla Morada (page 52)
Arroz a la Mexicana (page 64)
Refried Beans (page 71)
tortillas, shop-bought or
    homemade (page 57)
salt flakes

1. Preheat the grill (broiler) to maximum and line a roasting tray (pan) with tin (aluminum) foil.

2. Place all the ingredients for the green marinade in a food processor and process until well blended but still retaining some texture. Taste and adjust seasoning.

3. Lightly brush the prepared roasting tray with oil. Place the butterflied mackerel fillets on the tray. On each butterflied mackerel, spread one fillet with a quarter of the green marinade, and the other fillet with a quarter of the guajillo *adobo*, so that each mackerel has one green and one red fillet.

4. Place under the grill for 8–10 minutes, or until the mackerel is cooked. You might need to work in batches.

5. Arrange the cooked mackerel on a serving platter with lime wedges. Sprinkle with salt flakes and serve with the *Cebolla Morada*, rice, beans and warm tortillas on the side.

Squid in Creamy Chipotle Sauce

My mum usually prepares *calamares* (squid) in *mojo de ajo* with finely sliced guajillo chilli and fresh parsley. They are delicious and simple to prepare. I wanted to make this dish at home once, but I only had chipotle *adobo* rather than guajillo. I decided to add some creaminess by using leftover Pecorino cheese and cream. The result? A creamy, smoky, umami dish, and Natalie's favourite non-traditional recipe – one that I came up with completely by accident.

SERVES 4

850 g (1 lb 14 oz) squid (about 500 g/1 lb 2 oz once cleaned and prepared)
40 g (1½ oz) butter
2 garlic cloves, finely chopped
4–5 tablespoons Chipotle *en Adobo* Purée (page 82)
250 g (9 oz) *Crema* (page 65)
100 g (3½ oz) Pecorino cheese, grated

TO SERVE

cooked quinoa
Pico de Gallo (page 133)

1. To prepare the squid, detach the tentacles from the body by gently pulling them away, removing the entrails that are attached to the tentacles. Cut off the tentacles right below the eyes and remove the beak from the centre. Discard the entrails and beak. Pull on the skin that covers the body to remove it, and cut off the two fins. Cut the body into rings. Wash the rings, fins and tentacles. Dry them well – this will help them fry better.

2. Melt the butter in a large frying pan (skillet) over a low heat and slowly cook the garlic for 2–3 minutes. Increase the heat to medium, then add the squid and stir-fry for 3–4 minutes. Add the Chipotle *en Adobo* Purée and cook for another minute. Reduce the heat to low once more and add the cream and cheese. Let it simmer for a couple of minutes, stirring constantly, until the cheese has melted.

3. Serve at once with quinoa and *Pico de Gallo* on the side. I also like to serve a fresh baguette or sourdough loaf for dipping in the creamy sauce. Enjoy!

TIP: I like to make this recipe with the small squid called *chipirones*, as I find them more tender. The sauce is also delicious with prawns if you want to substitute.

Duck *Carnitas* with Tomatillo Ketchup

Carnitas are a classic from the state of Michoacán, whose cooks are famous for their big copper pots full of lard and pork simmering to make a confit. This recipe is a fusion of French and Mexican cooking. I really like duck confit because the meat is incredibly tasty and melts in the mouth. To cut the fattiness of the confit, I serve it here with a sweet and grassy tomatillo ketchup – surprisingly, this recipe works better with tinned tomatillos rather than fresh. To make the preparation of this dish easier, all the elements can be cooked in advance.

SERVES 4

FOR THE CONFIT DUCK LEGS
8 tablespoons salt flakes
4 duck legs
1 orange
35 g (1¼ oz) garlic cloves, peeled
6 sprigs of thyme
4 bay leaves
750 g (1 lb 10 oz) goose or duck
    fat, melted
1½ tablespoons soft light
    brown sugar
½ teaspoon salt

FOR THE TOMATILLO KETCHUP
2 tablespoons oil
3 apples, peeled, cored and sliced
790 g (1 lb 12 oz) tinned tomatillos,
    drained
1 cinnamon stick
60 g (2 oz/¼ cup) sugar
10 mint leaves
½ jalapeño chilli, chopped
1 tablespoon rice vinegar

FOR THE GARNISH
1 red onion
30 g (1 oz) coriander (cilantro),
    roughly chopped
15 g (½ oz) mint, roughly chopped
salt

1. Begin by preparing the duck legs. Sprinkle 4 tablespoons of the salt flakes over the bottom of a non-reactive container large enough to hold the legs in a single layer. Place the legs on top of the salt, skin side-up, pressing them down into the salt. Sprinkle the remaining salt flakes over the legs, pressing the salt into the skin. Cover and refrigerate for 3 hours.

2. After 3 hours, remove the legs from the salt, rinse and dry well. Place them in a sauté pan: they should fit it tightly in a single layer.

3. With a vegetable peeler, remove 8 long strips of zest from the orange and add them to the pan. Squeeze the orange and add the juice, then add the garlic, thyme sprigs and bay leaves. Cover with the melted goose fat. The legs should be completely immersed. Slowly bring to a bare simmer. Slow-cook for 2½ hours, until the meat falls easily from the bone.

4. Remove the orange zest strips from the fat and place in a small bowl. Add the soft brown sugar, salt and 4 teaspoons of the fat from the pan. Use a fork to crush into a paste and set aside. Let the legs cool in the fat. The confit will keep in its fat in the refrigerator for up to 1 week.

5. To make the tomatillo ketchup, heat the oil in a frying pan (skillet) over a medium heat. Add the apple slices and fry for 5 minutes until soft and caramelised. Meanwhile, place the drained tomatillos in a saucepan and cover with boiling water. Add the cinnamon stick and simmer for 15 minutes.

6. Drain the tomatillos and place in a blender, along with the apples. Add the sugar and blend until smooth, then pour into a saucepan and reduce the mixture over a low heat for 10 minutes until slightly thickened. Transfer back to the blender. Add the mint leaves, jalapeño and rice vinegar. Blend until smooth and let cool.

7. Preheat the oven to 200°C/180°C fan/400°F/gas mark 6. Remove the confit duck legs from the fat and place on a roasting tray (pan) lined with tin (aluminum) foil.

8. Spread the orange zest paste over the duck legs and bake for 15–20 minutes until golden and crisp.

9. Meanwhile, thinly slice the red onion and place in a bowl of salted water. When you are ready to serve, drain the onion and mix it in a bowl with the coriander and mint. Serve the duck legs with a few tablespoons of ketchup and a small handful of the garnish.

Chiles Rellenos

Ancho chillies are dried poblano chillies, and this dish is all about enjoying both the fresh chilli and its dried version. You can serve these stuffed chillies on a bed of *Caldillo de Jitomate*, or simply wrapped in a tortilla as a taco, commonly known as *tacos placeros*. The state of Puebla offers the best variety, in my opinion, especially at Hidalgo market. This is one of the most traditional dishes in Mexican cooking, with a simple Chihuahua or Ranchero cheese filling being one of the most popular. I grew up seeing my *Abuela* Carmela preparing these again and again. I hope you enjoy the smells of roasting poblano pepper at home as much as I do.

SERVES 4

3 tablespoons brown sugar

1 cinnamon stick

4 large or 8 medium-sized dried ancho chillies

4 large or 8 medium-sized poblano chillies

2–3 tablespoons grapeseed or vegetable oil

½ quantity *Caldillo de Jitomate* (page 51)

warm tortillas, shop-bought or homemade (page 57), to serve

FOR THE FILLING

1 small onion, finely chopped

3 garlic cloves, finely chopped

3 tablespoons grapeseed or vegetable oil

1 potato, peeled and diced

350 g (12 oz) minced (ground) beef

2 dried avocado leaves

pinch of ground cinnamon

3 ripe tomatoes, blended

1 tablespoon butter

½ plantain, peeled and diced

65 g (2¼ oz) raisins

20 g (¾ oz) almonds, toasted and chopped

20 g (¾ oz) pine nuts, toasted

¾ teaspoon salt

4 grinds of black pepper

1. Preheat the grill (broiler) to high.

2. Place the sugar and cinnamon stick in a large bowl and pour over 700 ml (24 fl oz/scant 3 cups) of boiling water. Stir until the sugar has dissolved, then add the dried chillies. They should be completely submerged, so place a weight on top, such as a plate or a bowl, if needed. Leave to soak for 15–30 minutes until the chillies are soft, then remove them from the liquid and cut a slit down one side of each chilli. Carefully remove the seeds, leaving the stem intact. Set aside.

3. Place the poblano chillies under the grill and grill for 20–40 minutes, depending on their size, turning them halfway through. They should be well charred. Place in a bowl, cover and set aside for about 30 minutes. The steam from the chillies will be trapped in the bowl, and this will help to loosen their skin. Once cool enough to handle, remove the skin and, just as you did with the dried chillies, cut a slit down the side of each one and remove the seeds, leaving the stem.

4. To prepare the filling, place a large sauté pan over a medium heat and fry the onion and garlic in the oil for 10–12 minutes until soft. Add the potato and fry for a further 5 minutes, until coloured. Increase the heat to medium–high and add the beef, in batches if necessary, cooking for 6–7 minutes until browned. Stir in the avocado leaves and cinnamon and cook for 1 minute. Add the blended tomatoes and stir well. Bring to a boil, then reduce the heat to low and simmer gently for 20 minutes.

5. Meanwhile, melt the butter in a small frying pan (skillet) over a low heat. Add the plantain and fry for 4–5 minutes. Add the raisins and cook for a couple of minutes until they are soft and puffed up. Add the plantain and raisins to the meat mixture, along with the nuts. Add the salt and pepper, then taste and adjust the seasoning if needed. Take off the heat and leave to cool.

6. Open up the chillies like little pouches and divide the filling between them. Close them up and flatten them in your hands. Heat the oil in a large frying pan over a low heat and gently cook the stuffed chillies for 7–8 minutes on each side. Meanwhile, reheat the *Caldillo de Jitomate*.

7. Serve the chillies on a bed of *caldillo*, with warm tortillas.

Ancho Rub Pot Chicken

Every cuisine has an iconic roast chicken dish. In our family, this ancho rub pot chicken is our stress-free Sunday lunch. It comes with a healthy coleslaw and a big bag of (less healthy) good-quality crisps. Roasted chickens – *pollos rostizados* – are normally sold in Mexico City right next to *panaderías*, which also sell pickled chillies, salsa and handmade crisps: comfort food to take away. To make your own, marinate the chicken overnight in the refrigerator and prepare the orange dressing in advance – that way, all you have to do on the day is shred vegetables and open a bag of crisps!

SERVES 4

1 orange
1.5 kg (3 lb 5 oz) whole chicken
20 g (¾ oz) fresh ginger root, peeled
4 garlic cloves, peeled
40 g (1½ oz) Ancho Dry Rub (page 85)
1 tablespoon olive oil

TO SERVE
a large packet of crisps – or 2!

FOR THE ORANGE COLESLAW DRESSING
6 tablespoons orange juice
2 tablespoons rice vinegar
2 tablespoons cider vinegar
1 teaspoon salt
1 tablespoon dark agave syrup
¼ teaspoon Mexican oregano
25 g (1 oz) red onion, thinly sliced

FOR THE COLESLAW
¼ red cabbage
¼ white cabbage
2 carrots, peeled
½ chayote (page 246)
10 g (¼ oz) coriander (cilantro) leaves

1. To prepare the chicken, juice the orange and transfer the juice to a bowl. Place the squeezed orange halves inside the chicken cavity. Grate half the ginger and 2 of the garlic cloves into the orange juice, then place the remaining ginger and garlic in the chicken cavity (no need to grate them).

2. Stir the ancho rub and olive oil into the mixture in the bowl to create a thick marinade, a bit thinner than a paste. Spread the marinade over the chicken and massage it both over and under the skin. Leave to marinate for at least one hour, or overnight.

3. Preheat the oven to 190°C/170°C fan/375°F/gas mark 5.

4. Place the chicken in a heavy casserole dish (Dutch oven) fitted with a lid. Cover and bake for 1 hour, then reduce the oven temperature to 170°C/150°C fan/340°F/gas mark 3½ and bake for another 20–25 minutes, or until cooked through. To check that the chicken in cooked, insert a digital thermometer in the thickest part of the leg. It should register 75°C (167°F). If you don't have a thermometer, pierce the chicken where one of the legs joins the body. If the juices run clear, the chicken is done. If not, cook for an extra 10 minutes and test again. Once cooked, remove the chicken from the casserole dish and leave to rest for 15 minutes.

5. While the chicken is cooking, prepare the coleslaw. Begin by mixing together all the dressing ingredients in a bowl. Leave to infuse while you prepare the vegetables.

6. Thinly slice both cabbages and place in a large bowl. Using a vegetable peeler, shred the carrot and chayote into thin ribbons and add these to the bowl too. Pour the dressing over the top and mix gently. Leave to infuse while the chicken is resting. Taste and adjust seasoning before serving.

7. Carve the chicken and serve with the coleslaw and crisps.

TIP: I like using the leftovers – if any! – the following day to prepare a chicken *torta*. Cut a *Telera* bun (page 63) and toast it with a little bit of butter. Spread over some Avocado Black Bean *Refritos* (page 71), Chipotle Mayonnaise (page 155) and a bit of coleslaw. Add some shredded chicken and a few avocado slices. When I was a child, I used to top the chicken with a few crisps to add some crunchiness, a school trick that was also allowed at my dinner table (I still occasionally do this!).

Ox Cheek *Suadero*

Tacos *de suadero* are an institution in Mexico City. The name *suadero* comes from a particularly tasty cut of beef located along the ribs that becomes meltingly soft when slowly cooked – but it is by no means the only meat that makes a taco *de suadero* so irresistible. Beef tripe, ox tongue, longaniza (the Mexican chorizo) or pigs' ears all join the *suadero* to be cooked into a confit in fat and cooking juices for hours in a special cooking pot called a *choricera*. This ingenious pan has a domed centre which rises above the fat, allowing you to reheat the tortillas and crispen the meats before serving.

I tried to keep this recipe simple, using only ox cheeks and chorizo, but you would make me very happy if you dropped in some tripe, ox tongue or a few pigs' ears. Keep the precious cooking fat to enhance fried eggs, onions, potatoes or vegetables.

SERVES 4–6

850 g (1 lb 14 oz) goose fat
2 ox cheeks (about 1 kg/2 lb 4 oz)
20 g (¾ oz) garlic cloves, peeled
6 sprigs of thyme
4 bay leaves
4 cooking chorizos
6 small cactus leaves in brine, rinsed and soaked in water overnight
8 calçot onions or spring onions (scallions), halved
about 20 tortillas, shop-bought or homemade (page 57)
salt flakes

TO SERVE

Salsa *Verde Cruda* (page 88)
fresh coriander (cilantro)
1 red onion, chopped

1. Heat 2 tablespoons of the goose fat in a large frying pan (skillet) over a medium heat and sear the ox cheeks on all sides for 2–3 minutes. Transfer to a heavy casserole dish (Dutch oven) over a low heat and cover with the rest of the goose fat and the garlic, thyme and bay leaves. Bring to a simmer and cook very gently for 3 hours. Add the chorizo and simmer for another hour. By now, the cheeks should be falling apart and easy to pull.

2. When the meat is almost ready, preheat the oven to 100°C/80°C fan/210°F/gas mark ¼. Drain the cactus leaves and pat dry with paper towels. Cut comb-like strips down the cactus paddles, but don't cut all the way. This will help the heat to penetrate the cactus.

3. Place a large non-stick frying pan over a low to medium heat. Add 1 tablespoon of the fat from the casserole dish and cook the calçot onions and cactus for 5–10 minutes, until well charred and tender. Transfer to an ovenproof dish and place in the oven to keep warm.

4. While the onions and cactus are cooking, remove the ox cheeks and chorizo from the fat and place in a bowl. Remove the skin from the chorizo and shred it with two forks. Shred the ox cheeks in the same manner.

5. In the same frying pan used for the onions and cactus, fry the chorizo over a medium heat for a couple of minutes, until a slight crust forms. Transfer to an ovenproof serving plate and keep warm in the oven. Repeat with the shredded ox cheeks: fry until crusty, season with salt flakes if needed, then transfer to the plate to keep warm in the oven.

6. Lightly brush the tortillas with some of the cooking fat from the casserole dish and, using the same frying pan as before, fry them in batches until soft and pliable. Wrap them in a clean kitchen towel or baking parchment to keep warm.

7. When you are ready to serve, arrange the meats, onions and cactus on a serving plate, and lay out the tortillas, along with the coriander leaves, chopped onion and salsa *verde cruda*. Let your guests assemble their own tacos, layering meat, charred vegetables and a drizzle of salsa over the top.

Oxtail
Mole de Olla

You will see big pots of *mole de olla* simmering slowly in Mexican markets. Somewhere between a soup and a stew, it is nourishing and usually made with cheap cuts of beef and a mixture of vegetables that almost always includes potatoes and corn. I really like the flavour oxtail gives to this stew. You can slow-cook the meat ahead of time and leave it in the refrigerator overnight, then skim the fat off the top and finish cooking the stew with the vegetables on the day.

SERVES 4

3 guajillo chillies, trimmed and
    deseeded
3 pasilla mixe chillies, trimmed
    and deseeded
250 ml (8½ fl oz/1 cup) boiling water
500 g (1 lb 2 oz) ripe tomatoes,
    roughly chopped
1 onion, chopped
8 garlic cloves, peeled
1.5 kg (3 lb 5 oz) oxtail, chopped
3 tablespoons oil
750 ml (25 fl oz/3 cups) water
2 sweetcorn cobs, each cut into
    6 pieces
300 g (10 oz) red potatoes, skin left
    on, cubed
1 chayote (page 246), cubed
120 g (4 oz) green beans, trimmed

1. Place all the chillies in a *comal* or non-stick frying pan (skillet) over a medium heat and toast them for a few minutes until soft and pliable. Be careful not to burn them. Transfer them to a bowl and cover with the boiling water. Leave to soften for 1 hour.

2. Place the tomatoes, onion and garlic in a blender and add chillies, along with their soaking water. Blend until very smooth, then set aside.

3. Heat the oil in a large casserole dish (Dutch oven) over a low to medium heat. Add the oxtail and fry for 5 minutes, turning often, until well browned on all sides. Pour the blended chilli mixture over the top. Add 750 ml (25 fl oz/3 cups) of water and simmer, covered, for 2 hours. Remove the lid and simmer for another hour, or until the stock is slightly thickened and the meat easily falls off the bone.

4. Skim off some of the coloured oil suspended on the surface. Add the sweetcorn pieces and potatoes and simmer for 15 minutes, then add the chayote and beans and simmer for a further 20 minutes, or until all the vegetables are tender.

5. Serve hot in a bowl. Add some lime juice into the *mole de olla* and accompained with fresh tortillas.

Pork Chops al Pastor

As you will know if you are a *taqueria* addict, the pork *al pastor* is grilled (broiled) on a rotating *trompo*, or spit. Thin slices are shaved off the grilled sides to fill the tortillas. You can reproduce the *pastor* experience at home by piling up pork chops, securing them with a kebab skewer and slicing off the sides. Two key ingredients form the pillars of tacos *al pastor*: the achiote paste in the marinade and the grilled pineapple added on top. Achiote paste is a mixture of crushed annatto seeds (page 133) and spices. As well as giving the marinade an intense red tone, it brings a unique nutty, almost citrusy flavour. For the taco topping, I like to grill slices of pineapple and marinate them in brown sugar and lime.

In Mexico City, there is a lot of debate around who created the *pastor* taco recipe. I remember going to El Tizoncito in Condesa borough with my parents and sister for a real treat when we were in the area. It was always exciting as a child to see the *taqueros* slicing the meat thinly from top to bottom of the rotating *trompo* and then, very quickly, cutting a slice of pineapple at the very top of the meat, which would inevitably fly all the way to the plate held by another *taquero* about 1 metre (3 feet) away, with such precision that you could be forgiven for thinking this was the main reason for our excitement – until the pineapple and pork would melt in your mouth. Their knife skills are absolutely unique.

SERVES 4

4 pork chops
30 g (1 oz/2½ tablespoons)
    light brown sugar
1 pineapple
juice of 1 lime
1 grilled jalapeño chilli
1 grilled Scotch bonnet chilli

FOR THE PASTOR MARINADE

15 g (½ oz) guajillo chillies, trimmed
    and deseeded
3 árbol chillies, trimmed and
    deseeded
10 g (½ oz) ancho chillies, trimmed
    and deseeded
75 ml (2¼ fl oz/⅓ cup) water
35 g (1¼ oz) achiote paste
1 tablespoon salt
2 tablespoons cider vinegar
5 teaspoons rice vinegar
¾ teaspoon ground cinnamon
½ teaspoon coriander seeds
125 ml (4¼ fl oz/½ cup) pineapple
    juice
125 ml (4¼ fl oz/½ cup) apple juice
20 g (¾ oz) garlic cloves, peeled
2 tablespoons agave syrup

TO SERVE

1 red onion, halved and thinly
    sliced, to garnish
warm tortillas, to serve

1. Begin by preparing the marinade. Toast the chillies in a *comal* or non-stick frying pan (skillet) over a medium to high heat for a few minutes until fragrant, being careful not to burn them. Transfer the toasted chillies to a bowl, cover with water and leave for at least 1 hour to soften.

2. Drain the chillies, reserving 75 ml (2½ fl oz/⅓ cup) of their soaking water. Place the drained chillies and reserved soaking water in a blender, then add the rest of the marinade ingredients and blend until very smooth.

3. Place the pork chops in a non-reactive bowl and cover with the marinade, making sure the chops are well coated. Leave in the refrigerator overnight.

4. Remove the marinated pork chops out from the refrigerator at least 1 hour before cooking them to bring them up to room temperature.

5. Preheat the oven to 190°C/170°C fan/375°F/gas mark 5 and line a baking tray (pan) with baking parchment. Scatter the sugar on a plate.

6. Holding the pineapple by its leaves, remove the peel and eyes with a knife, then square it off by cutting off 4 big chunks along its fibrous core. Cut each chunk into slices 1 cm (½ in) thick.

7. Heat a non-stick griddle pan over a low to medium heat and griddle the pineapple slices for 10–15 minutes on each side until well-grilled and tender. You'll need to work in batches. Dip each grilled slice in the brown sugar to coat, then place in a bowl. Season with lime juice and set aside.

8. Keeping the griddle pan on the heat, add the pork chops and cook for 3 minutes on each side, then place them on the prepared baking tray. Place in the oven and bake for 6–8 minutes, depending on the thickness of the chops.

9. When you are ready to serve, pile the chops on top of each other, then stack the pineapple slices on top of the chops. Finish with the two grilled chillies and thread a kebab skewer through the middle of the whole pile to secure. Cut thin slices of pork and pineapple directly from the pile and serve in warm tortillas, garnished with slices of red onion.

Pibil-style Pork Ribs

Cochinita pibil is the emblematic dish of Yucatan. *Cochinita*, the whole suckling pig, is doused in achiote marinade, wrapped in banana leaves and slow-roasted in a pit. I have already mentioned that annatto seeds are used as a natural colouring in the food industry (page 133). Achiote paste, a mix of crushed annatto seeds and spices, has a deep, vibrant red colour and a unique peppery, musky flavour which pairs beautifully with pork. In Yucatan, sour oranges are used for the marinade. Try this with the bitter juices of Seville oranges, or mix together orange and lime juice. This marinade works particularly well with spare ribs. If you can get hold of banana leaves, they will add extra flavour, but the ribs can still be slow-cooked to succulence simply wrapped in baking parchment and foil.

A word of warning: the habanero chillies used in the marinade and the *Xni' Pek* salsa give these spare ribs a good kick.

SERVES 4–6

2 x 1 kg (2 lb 4 oz) racks of pork ribs
oil, for brushing

FOR THE *PIBIL* MARINADE
150 g (5 oz) achiote paste,
  crumbled
230 ml (7¾ fl oz/scant 1 cup) freshly
  squeezed orange juice
3 tablespoons lime juice
45 g (1½ oz) garlic cloves
1 habanero chilli, trimmed
1½ teaspoons Mexican oregano
¾ teaspoon salt

TO SERVE
½ quantity Black Beans with
  Avocado Leaves (page 68)
Xni' Pek salsa (page 97)

1. Place all the ingredients for the marinade in a blender and blend until smooth. Place the ribs in a large non-reactive container – a glass or porcelain dish is best. Cover with the marinade and leave in the refrigerator overnight.

2. Remove the ribs from the refrigerator about 1 hour before cooking them. Preheat the oven to 160°C/140°C fan/325°F/gas mark 3 and line a roasting tray (pan) with a large piece of tin (aluminum) foil, big enough to enclose the ribs. Place a large sheet of baking parchment on top of the foil, then place the ribs on the baking parchment. Scrape out any marinade left in the dish and pour it over the top of the ribs, along with 200 ml (7 fl oz/scant 1 cup) of water. Cover with a second piece of baking parchment and wrap the ribs in the paper and foil. Crumple the edges of the foil to seal.

3. Place in the oven and bake for 2 hours, then open the foil and paper and check that the meat is well cooked and is falling off the bone. Increase the oven temperature to 180°C/160°C fan/350°F/gas mark 5. Lightly brush the ribs with oil and bake for a further 20 minutes, in the open parcel, until the top of the meat has a slight crust.

4. Serve straight from the oven, with black beans and *Xni' Pek* salsa on the side.

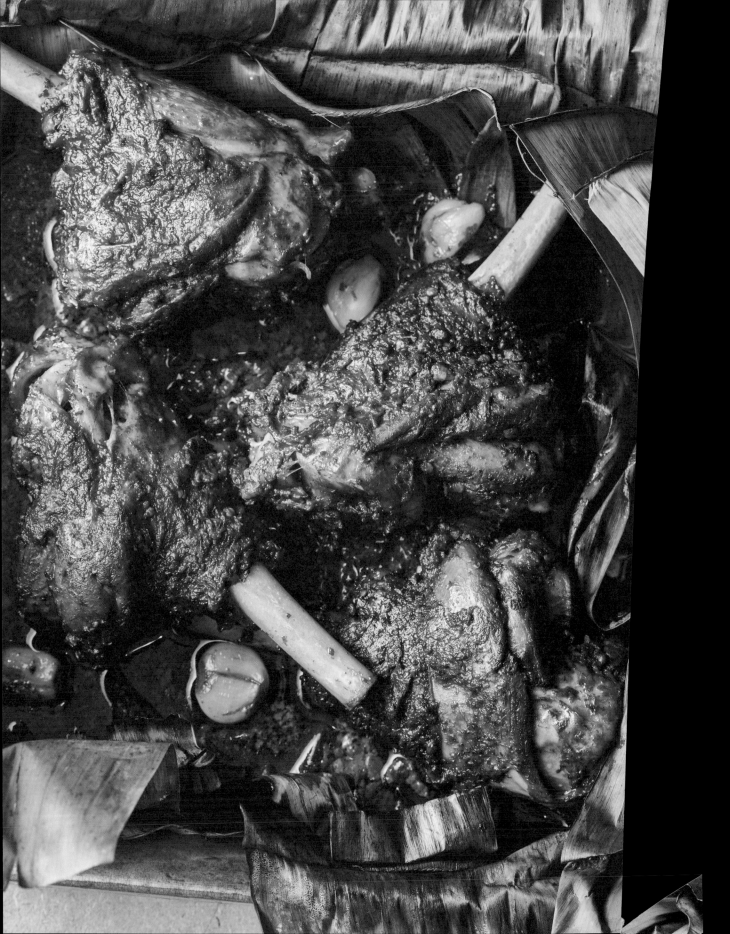

FOR THE *PIPIÁN VERDE*

100 g (3½ oz) pumpkin seeds, toasted
100 g (3½ oz) tinned tomatillos
100 g (3½ oz) tinned tomatillo brine
20 g (¾ oz) onion
8 g (¼ oz) tarragon leaves
12 mint leaves
5 large Thai basil leaves
1 tablespoon grapeseed or vegetable oil
40 g (1½ oz) spinach
450 ml (15 fl oz/1¾ cups) boiling water
1 jalapeño chilli, trimmed and chopped
¾ teaspoon salt
10 g (¼ oz) coriander (cilantro) leaves

6. Arrange the celeriac wedges on the prepared tray and brush with the oil. Bake for 20 minutes, then add the mushrooms to the tray and bake for another 10–15 minutes, until the celeriac is tender but still a bit crunchy. Remove from the oven. Once cool enough to handle, dice the celeriac and mushrooms.

7. Place the *pipián verde* in a saucepan over a low heat and gently warm through.

8. Meanwhile, place a frying pan (skillet) over a medium–high heat and fry the *sofrito* and oil for a couple of minutes. Add the diced celeriac and mushroom and stir-fry for another minute. Add the spinach and cook until just wilted.

9. Lightly brush the tortillas with oil and, in a separate frying pan, fry for 1 minute on each side, until soft and pliable.

10. You can serve this dish in two different ways. You can dip the tortillas in the sauce and place on a plate, then cover half of each tortilla with about 40 g (1½ oz) of the celeriac and mushroom mixture, before folding and repeating with the other tortillas; or you can simply fill and fold the tortillas, and spoon the sauce over the top. Serve, garnished with pumpkin seeds.

Glossary

ACHIOTE Yucatecan paste made from ground annatto seeds and spices with a very vibrant, red colour. Traditionally used to marinade pork for *cochinta pibil* by diluting this paste with orange juice from a local orange variety called naranja agria.

ADOBO A smoky, chilli-based paste made with onions, garlic and other spices.

AGAVE A native Mexican plant with broad, flat leaves that come to a point on the end and grow a single tall flower at maturity. The heart of the blue agave plant (*piña*) is used to make high quality tequila.

AL PASTOR Meat (any type but usually pork) cooked over a spit, Middle Eastern-style.

ANCHO Sundried poblano pepper.

ARBOL A small, fiery red chilli.

ASADO/ASADA Grilled (broiled) meat, e.g. *carne asada* is meat broiled over hot coals.

AVOCADO LEAVES The leaves of an avocado plant, they have a slight anise flavour, and are often used in *guisados* (stews) and *adobos* (marinades).

BARBACOA Usually meat, traditionally lamb, cooked in an underground pit, often wrapped in agave or banana leaves.

BURRITO A flour toritilla softened with heat and wrapped around a number of ingredients (usually meat and beans) to form a tight, cylindrical parcel. Often associated with 'Tex-Mex', it can contain a variety of ingredients and range in sizes.

CALCOTS A type of spring onion (scallion) often found in Spain that is size-wise somewhere between a spring onion and a small leek.

CARNITAS A Mexican food speciality of the Michoacán region. *Carnitas* is essentially confit pork – pork cuts, cooked in lard – and recipes often include Mexican Coca-Cola and orange juice.

CEVICHE Raw fish cured in citrus juices and mixed traditionally with tomatoes, onions, chillies and herbs.

CHAYOTE A type of squash.

CHICHARRONES Deep fried pork rinds.

CHILAQUILES Totopos (AKA tortilla chips) traditionally topped with salsa *verde* or *roja* as well as *crema* and cheese.

CHIPOTLE Dried, smoked jalapeño chilli.

CHORIZO Fresh, highly seasoned sausage flavoured with chillies and spices.

COCA-COLA (MEXICAN) Also known as 'Mexi-coke', unlike the US version of Coca-Cola, the Mexican format is sweetened with cane sugar rather than high fructose corn syrup, garnering its flavour more 'natural' tasting with a complexity and richness of herbs and spices. Mexican Coke is often included in cooking recipes across Mexico, particularly when using fatty meats.

COTIJA This firm cow's milk cheese presents a pale and crumbly texture, with a savoury richness similar to Parmesan or pecorino cheese. It is cage ripened and an officially recognised regional speciality from the Michoacan region in Mexico.

ELOTE Fresh corn on the cob.

ENCHILADAS Lightly fried corn tortilla dipped in sauce or *mole* and traditionally stuffed with shredded chicken or beef, but can also be with cheese and vegetables.

EPAZOTE A wild herb that grows all over North America. Used to flavour Mexican dishes, soups and stews.

ESCABECHE Mixture of oil, vinegar, herbs and seasonings used to pickle jalapeños and other vegetables.

FLAUTA A large corn tortilla usually filled with beef, chicken or slightly smashed potato then rolled and deep fried until crisp. It takes this name because of its flute-like shape.

GUAJILLO The d... ...rsion of a mirasol chilli, guaj... ...e sweet and fruity with a mild h...

GUISADOS A meat or vege... stew, slow cooked until ingre... soften and break down.

HABANERO Very spicy, fruity and aromatic chilli pepper very popular in Yucatecan cooking.

HORCHATA Soft drink made by blending ground rice with water and spices including cinnamon or cardamom.

HUITLACOCHE In Mexico, *huitlacoche* is a Mexican food delicacy to be savoured. Also called corn smut, maize mushroom or Mexican truffle.

JALAPEÑO A medium-hot fresh chilli pepper very popular in Mexican food. Jalapeños are also known as chipotles in their dehydrated form.

MASA Dough of nixtamalised and ground corn kernels mixed with water used to make corn tortillas and many different *antojitos*. It also refers to the dough made with nixtamalised corn *masa harina*, water and salt to prepare tortillas.

MEXICAN OREGANO A commonly used herb that has citrusy, grassy notes.

MEZCAL Distilled liquor made from the juice of several types of agaves – wild and harvested – after being pit roasted and cooked.

MOJO DE AJO Confit garlic sauce.

MOLCAJETE Stone mortar used mostly to grind chillies for salsas.

MOLE A very complex sauce in Mexican cooking traditionally made with chillies, spices and herbs. *...ole poblano* is probably one of ... ...ost well known moles and it ... ...nd balances chillies, spices, ...etables, chocolate and se...

MOR... ...OTLE A slightly smoked ... ...y dried jalapeño chilli. Com... ...wn as chipotle morita.

MECO CHIPOT... ...ed and dried jalapeño ... ...a deep smokey and to... ...ur. Commonly known as ... ...co.

NIXTAMALIZATION The ... of soaking and cooking drie... kernels with an alkaline solutio... commonly known as limewater. Nixtamal is the product obtained after this process and when grounded it is turned into corn *masa*. This is an ancient process utilised in Mexico and Central America to produce corn tortillas and other maize-based products.

PAMBAZO A Mexican dish made from special bread dipped in a red guajillo pepper sauce and filled with potato, chorizo, lettuce and cream.

PASILLA MIXE Long, thin, almost black chilli with a very deep smokey flavour only produced in the Mixe region of Oaxaca.

PIQUIN POWDER A hot chilli powder made from piquin peppers.

POBLANO Dark green, rounded fresh chilli used for *chile rellenos*.

POZOLE Robust, medium spicy soup with pork or chicken, hominy, onions and spices. Also called *posole*.

SERRANO One of northern Mexico's most commonly used chillies. Small, green and very hot.

TACO Usually a corn tortilla, folded in half and filled with meat, vegetables and salsa. Can be fried and served crispy or grilled (broiled) and served soft and topped with a variety of ingredients.

TAMALES Corn dough filled with meat, vegetables or fruit, wrapped up traditionally in a corn husk or banana leaves and steamed.

TOMATILLO A relative of the gooseberry family. Resembles a small green tomato, it is very flavoursome and used in many salsas, well known ... the main ingredient is salsa *verde*.

TO... ...A Mexican style hot or cold ... ...h on a bread roll traditionally ... ...ra.

TO... ...t, thin and circular disc made ... ...lised dough and then co... ...*comal* or *plancha*. Probably ... ...portant food in Mexican co...

TOSTADA Crisp... ...orn tortilla, often topp... ...*sados* (stews).

TOTOPOS Traditional r... ...d tortilla chips.

Index

Image descriptions

Page 4. Lady rushing but smiling on her way to deliver *comida corrida* near Mercado de San Juan, México City. No Deliveroo needed.
– Edson Diaz-Fuentes

Page 6. Picture of Ciudad de México traditional sign made by Melquiades García Alcántara of AKA Rotulacion Artesanal. This type of lettering and design gained a lot of popularity in Mexico City in the 70s and 80s among *taquerias, torterias,* ice cream parlours and *paleterías* primarily. Mr Alcántara calculates he had made over 7,500 metres (24,600 feet) of signs in the last 50 years decorating key establishments in the city.
– Montserrat Castro

Page 15. Dulcería de Celaya in 5 de Mayo St, Historic Center, Mexico City. One of the few remain shops for traditional and authentic Mexican sweets in México City.
– Edson Diaz-Fuentes

Page 16. Our first picture taken outside Santo Remedio Restaurant in London Bridge back in 2017.
– Ronaldo Tavares

Page 18. Fish monger from the Triakidae family showing cazón in Mercado de San Juan. Cazón is widely used fish in Mexico known in English as snapper or soupfin shark from the Triakidae family.
– Edson Diaz-Fuentes

Page 20. Los Cocuyos Taqueria at 2am. Bolivar 57 Historic Center, Mexico City.
– Edson Diaz-Fuentes

Page 26. Dried chillies shop in Puebla.
– Edson Diaz-Fuentes

Page 29. Clay Pot full of *mole poblano* ingredients ready to turn into a paste. As part of mole workshop by Liz Galicia at Mural de los Poblanos back in 2014.
– Edson Diaz-Fuentes

Page 34, 35, 36 & 37. Gerardo Soriano and his family preparing *barbacoa* in

San José de los Laureles, Morelos. From choosing and killing the sheep, cleaning it and preparing the *hoyo* for the underground oven for hours the family prepare all stages of this process. They then cook the meat covered in maguey and avocado leaves overnight for about 12 hours.
– Adam Wiseman

Page 94. Pasilla mixe chilli seller in Central de Abastos in Oaxaca. Probably the only chilli that is not widely use in Mexico City dishes and cooking, but an essential in my cupboard since I discovered it almost two decades ago.
– Edson Diaz-Fuentes

Page 110. Restaurante El Cardenal, Calle de la Palma 23, Historic Center Mexico City.
– Edson Diaz-Fuentes

Page 167. *Carniceria.*
– Edson Diaz-Fuentes

Page 195. *Polleria.*
– Edson Diaz-Fuentes

About the Author

Edson Diaz-Fuentes was born and raised in Mexico City. He realised he was not quite like the others among his friends when he would spend time from a young age observing meticulously how food was made, served and presented. Whether at his grandmother's house, at a *taqueria* or at restaurants for family celebrations he found himself mesmerised by the process of bringing food to fruition. Edson has spent time living in New York, London and Oaxaca City. It was in Oaxaca where he spent time in the kitchen of Alejandro Ruiz, at Casa Oaxaca, learning about the diversity of some of Mexico's most treasured ingredients and its slow food cooking techniques. Edson set up Santo Remedio in London in 2015 with his wife Natalie to recreate the flavours he grew up with in Mexico. What started off as an idea in New York and later a food stall in Shoreditch, East London, evolved into a critically acclaimed restaurant, now situated in London Bridge. Edson enjoys travelling in Mexico discovering new food, flavours and ingredients as well as the stories and traditions behind the dishes he tries. He particularly enjoys getting lost in markets anywhere he visits. Edson lives in London with his wife Natalie, son Sebastian and daughter Cecilia, and also spends his time between Cornwall and Oaxaca.

www.edsondiazfuentes.com

Acknowledgements

I embarked on writing this cookbook just as the Covid-19 pandemic and first lockdown started in London in March 2020. I had just begun to develop recipes when I lost my sense of taste and smell, which was a challenge to say the least! Thankfully it was short lived. All the family was at home due to lockdown, the restaurant was closed and the uncertainty for the hospitality industry was unprecedented. It was definitely not how I envisaged my time cooking and writing. But amidst the political chaos, u-turns and confusion both in the UK and Mexico I finally got to work creating the recipes and stories for this book. Good food and social interaction is now more important than ever. And as I write this from Mexico, I am in awe of all the resilience of country's food producers and suppliers. They keep going in the face of all the challenges due to the pandemic, a year on from when it started. Special thanks to all those men and women who have been behind the *comales*, pots and *trompos* that are part of Mexico's street food scene. They have inspired me without knowing it, bite after bite. I am extremely grateful to all those involved in making this book happen. Thanks for your honest feedback and input. You know who you are. To my *Chilango* and New Yorker friend Richard Ampudia for the countless chats about Mexican food and how to make it possible outside Mexico one taco at a time. To Adam Wiseman for capturing the essence of DF with his wonderful photography. To my parents and grandparents who introduced me to the wonders of Mexico food. To our restaurant managers Celine, Alexandra and Daniel for their contribution to Santo Remedio in our mission to bring the very best Mexican food and hospitality to the UK. To the team at Hardie Grant - Eve, Valerie, Rachel, Rob, Daniel and all those who have helped bring this book to life. Particular thanks goes to my wife and talented journalist Natalie, for hoovering up all the *antojitos* at home but most importantly for helping me when I had writer's block. And thank you to my harshest critics, my son Sebastian and daughter Cecilia, for taste testing the non-spicy recipes in the book. The *tamales* and juices are all the better, thanks to the faces you made upon trying them!

Published in 2021 by Hardie Grant Books,
an imprint of Hardie Grant Publishing

Hardie Grant Books (London)
5th & 6th Floors
52–54 Southwark Street
London SE1 1UN

Hardie Grant Books (Melbourne)
Building 1, 658 Church Street
Richmond, Victoria 3121

hardiegrantbooks.com

All rights reserved. No part of this publication may be reproduced, stored in a retrieval
system or transmitted in any form by any means, electronic, mechanical, photocopying,
recording or otherwise, without the prior written permission of
the publishers and copyright holders.

The moral rights of the author have been asserted.

Copyright text © Edson Diaz-Fuentes
Copyright Photography © Robert Billington, Edson Diaz-Fuentes, Adam Wiseman

British Library Cataloguing-in-Publication Data. A catalogue record for this book is
available from the British Library.

Ciudad de Mexico
ISBN: 978-1-78488-393-5

10 9 8 7 6 5 4 3 2 1

Publisher: Kajal Mistry
Commissioning Editor: Eve Marleau
Design and Illustration: Daniel New
Photographer: Robert Billington and Adam Wiseman
Food Stylist: Valerie Berry
Prop Stylist: Rachel Vere
Copy-editor: Tara O'Sullivan
Proofreader: Gillian Haslam
Indexer: Vanessa Bird
Production Controller: Nikolaus Ginelli

Colour reproduction by p2d
Printed and bound in China by Leo Paper Products Ltd.

MIX
Paper from
responsible sources
FSC™ C020056
FSC
www.fsc.org

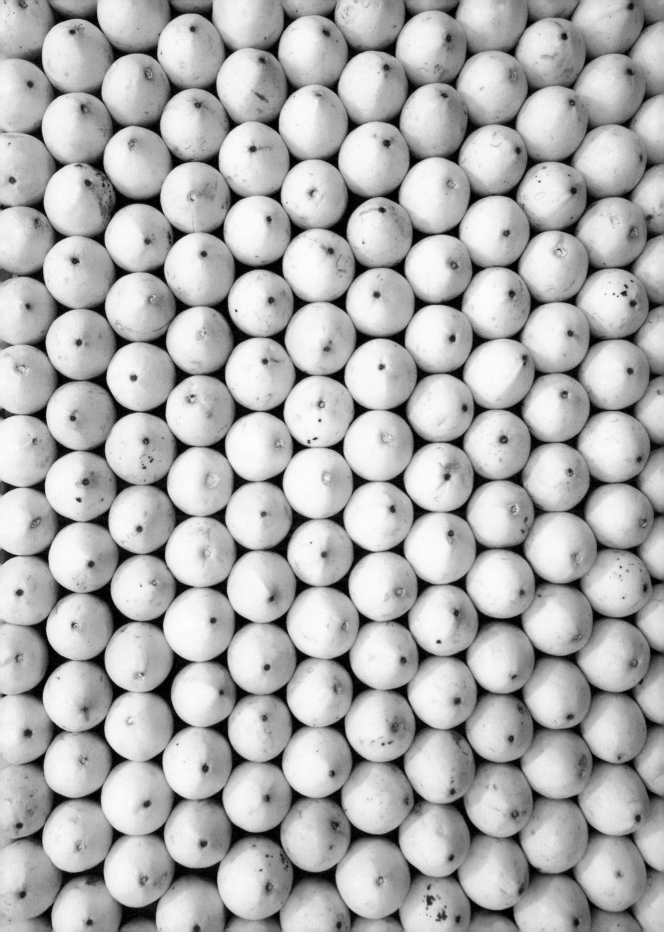